RITA F. SNOWDEN

DISCOVERIES THAT DELIGHT

A fresh love of the Psalms

Collins
FOUNT PAPERBACKS

First published by Fount Paperbacks,
London in 1982

Made and printed in Great Britain by
William Collins Sons & Co. Ltd, Glasgow

DISCOVERIES THAT DELIGHT

Rita F. Snowden is widely known in many countries and is the author of more than sixty books for adults and children. After six years in business she trained as a deaconess of the New Zealand Methodist Church, serving in turn two pioneer country areas before moving to the largest city for several years of social work during an economic depression.

Miss Snowden has served the world Church, beyond her own denomination, with regular broadcasting commitments. She has written and spoken in Britain, Canada, the United States, in Australia, and in Tonga at the invitation of Queen Salote. She has represented her church at the World Methodist Conference in Oxford; later being elected the first woman Vice-President of the New Zealand Methodist Church, and President of its Deaconess Association. She is an Honorary Vice-President of the New Zealand Women Writers' Society, a Fellow of the International Institute of Arts and Letters, and a member of P.E.N.

Miss Snowden has been honoured by the award of the Order of the British Empire, and by the citation of 'The Upper Room' in America.

Her most recent books are *Prayers for Busy People*, *Christianity Close to Life*, *Bedtime Stories and Prayers* (for children) and *I Believe Here and Now*.

Books by the same author available in Fount Paperbacks

BEDTIME STORIES AND PRAYERS
(for children)
CHRISTIANITY CLOSE TO LIFE
I BELIEVE HERE AND NOW
MORE PRAYERS FOR WOMEN
PRAYERS FOR BUSY PEOPLE
PRAYERS FOR THE FAMILY
PRAYERS IN LATER LIFE
A WOMAN'S BOOK OF PRAYERS

Rita Snowden also edited
IN THE HANDS OF GOD
by William Barclay

Dedicated
to
My Home-sharing Friend,
Rene

Contents

Preface

Two human powers for which I give constant thanks, are my capacities *for discovery and for delight*. It is curious that few expect to find them together in religion. But the Psalmist's expression that sets the spirit of this book, is: 'I delight to do Thy Will, O my God!' (Psalm 40:8, AV).

Discovered in youth, in the middle years, or in the milder days of maturity, there is nothing to match it.

R.F.S.

A Favourite Psalm Missing

Long before ever I set foot in Ceylon, or in the islands of Fiji and Tonga, whither I had gone as a guest-speaker, I was fortunate to hear of Canon Tristram's misadventure. As an authority on Bible backgrounds, he was invited to stop off in Ceylon, on his way by ship to India. Asked to lead in worship, as he had no Sinhalese he had need of an interpreter. And to make sure that all would be well, he chose what he thought of as a simple Psalm: the Twenty-third. But those twin provisions were not enough.

When the Canon had finished speaking, his interpreter asked him: 'Sir, do you mind if I say something to you?' And given gracious permission, he went on. 'Sir, are you aware that no one in this island has ever seen a sheep?' It suddenly, and painfully, dawned upon their visiting speaker that by the same circumstance, they had never had dealings with a shepherd. So the cherished Psalm that he had counted as simple, had for them lost much of its beauty and meaning.

It was now the Canon's turn to ask a question: 'And what did you do about the translation?' For answer, he was told: 'Oh, I turned it into a buffalo that had lost its calf!'

Knowing this, it need not surprise any one of us to learn that the opening words of the Twenty-third Psalm are rendered in Lapland: 'The Lord is my reindeer-keeper' – because there are no sheep there.

Sadly, the last book to come from my long-time friend, Dr William Barclay, although described by the publisher, Collins, as 'Expositions of Selected Psalms', and entitled *The Lord is My Shepherd*, does not have a section on the Twenty-third. That favourite Psalm is missing altogether. But it is not for lack of knowledge as a scholar, or sensibility as a famous speaker, broadcaster and preacher – it was simply that death caught up with the Doctor before he could complete his work on the Psalms. So there are only five after the introduction 'Approaching the Psalms': Psalm 1: 'A Good Man'; Psalm 2: 'God is the Lord'; Psalm 8: 'God and Man'; Psalm 19: 'God's Plan'; and Psalm 104: 'God's World'. (I wonder what my friend would think of this last book, bearing as it does the original title *The Lord is My Shepherd*, but without any reference to this widely favourite Psalm.) Dr Barclay, son of Scotland, lived in a land where sheep and shepherds were important, as I do; here in New Zealand we have many times more sheep than we have people. 'Before his death,' I am assured on the flap of his book, 'the author was hoping to complete a presentation of all the Psalms.' So my loss must be borne.

Of course, he was strictly a New Testament scholar – with a genius for clear, simple exposition. On my shelves are pink-jacketed copies of each book of the New Testament, under the general title *Daily Study Bible*. I was amused to learn from him how it began. 'The Publications Manager of our Church of Scotland,' said he, 'came to me one day, and asked bluntly enough: "Would you be prepared to do us a volume of daily Bible readings, as a stopgap, until we get someone decent to do them for us?"' With a laugh, as we shared our meal together, he went on: 'I immediately agreed. When the first volume was coming to an end they still were without "someone decent". So I did a second, and so on and on, until *the whole of the New Testament had been covered.*'

And now – having scanned missionary bookshelves around the world, and more than once also ministerial bookshelves, not to mention those of countless laity, youth leaders, and ageing lovers of the Book – I marvel at the widespread ministry of these little pink commentaries. And many, I observe, are as well-handled and worn as my own.

A Favourite Psalm Missing

For eleven years, William Barclay was Professor of Divinity and Biblical Criticism at Glasgow University; and, amongst other things, a member of the Advisory Committee working on the New English Bible, and a member of the Apocrypha Panel of Translators. But he never apologized for his simplicity. On my shelf, at arm's length, is a copy of his *New Testament, Volume 1: The Gospels and the Acts of the Apostles*. That new translation in two volumes is a handsome possession, all the more so because it came to me as a gift from him, bearing a note: 'Herewith the translation. I send it to you with every good wish, and with gratitude for all that you and your work have meant to me for the last thirty years and more.' We exchanged many books, and gave each other permission to quote; he chaired an important meeting for me in Scotland, when I was called to speak; he begged me never to visit Scotland on any of my journeys without taking the opportunity to share talk over a meal. So generous was he – I owe him so much! I feel it a real loss, not to have in his last book from our mutual publishers, Collins, a clear commentary on this favourite Psalm, the Twenty-third.

Apart from life adding colour and significance to its words, I find the reverse is true – knowledge of the Shepherd and His sheep can add meaning to many a simple experience in this life. I never go to Britain without spending some time in the Cotswolds – sheep country. I love every inch of its blue sky overhead in Spring, its winding roads, and green grass between white-faced houses of native stone, that look to me what they truly are, snug homes. The poet's heart surely grasped the right words when he wrote:

These homes, these valleys spread below me here,
  These rooks, the tilted stacks, the beasts in pen
Have been the heartfelt thing, past speaking dear,
  To unknown generations of dead men,

Who century after century held these farms
And looking out to watch the changing sky
Heard, as we hear, the rumours and alarms
Of war at hand, and danger passing nigh.

For this is sheep country. As early as the twelfth century, Flemish traders were coming for Cotswold wool, and in the fourteenth century Florentine merchants were competitors in the markets. In the fifteenth century, that Cotswold wool – from a breed of sheep thereabouts, one of the very oldest in England – was widely sought. In 1401, in his own church where he now rests, one sheep-man, William Grevel, is described on his brass as 'the Flower of the Woolmerchants of all England'.

Many of these men grew rich, and, loving God and beautiful things, built and endowed many of the lovely churches that still stand there beneath the skies.

I was staying in the climbing hill town of Burford, when one morning I stepped along to the office of the sub-editor of *The Countryman*, that chubby, green magazine, full of green, growing thoughts. He told me, over a mug of coffee, that there still remained one flock of Cotswold sheep in the country, a few miles off. So I made it part of that Spring morning to go out there.

As I turned my little car from my lodging in old Burford, a blackbird on a green-tipped branch was trying over a few phrases. After the exceptionally long, wet Winter, binding the housewife to her chores, and hindering the man of the soil, this was a welcome sign. Over all, at long last, was a blue sky, and on the high places pure, bracing airs. To borrow the words of Robert Henriques – a man who had lived in the Cotswolds for years – 'It is country, a poem, an enchantment, an inevitable accident. It is all these, and many more.' It defies analysis. The highest parts reach nine hundred feet above sea-level, whilst a hundred little villages are tucked away down beside limpid streams, sheltered by great trees. And there are gracious, bare, sweeping places, where the furrows of the patient ploughman come down over the slope with the generosity of the season.

Seeking the shepherd and his flock, I eventually found myself in the little village of Aldsworth. There was scarcely a soul about. Then the postwoman put in an appearance, pushing her bicycle, carrying her mailbag from door to door. And, after a greeting, I got directions to the home of the owner of the flock. Presently I knocked at his door. But it did not surprise me on such a lovely morning, after such a spell of miserable weather, that he was not at home.

Whilst I was wondering what to do next, a housewife, with a brown-paper parcel and a packet of tea, came along. I told her what a wonderful morning it was – and she told *me* what a wonderful morning it was! When I made known my purpose, to my great surprise, she said: 'I'm the wife of Mr Garne's shepherd! He's over with the flock just now, where it's grazing, but he'll be home soon for his lunch. Would you like to come in, and wait for him?' I thanked her, but told her: 'No. I'd sooner go over to where he is – I want to see the sheep.' She kindly directed me, and with her help, I went on my way, back on the road along which I had come, then over a stone wall, and another and another.

And, casting my eyes around, there I saw the old shepherd, tall and grey-haired, standing among his little flock – a mere handful of beautiful sheep. I told him where I came from, and of my interest in his flock.

'I'm more 'an pleased to show 'em,' was his encouraging response. At the gateway that gave entrance to where we stood, I noticed the hard mud, indented deeply with footmarks now baked dry, reminding me of the hard Winter. Nor had early Spring, so far, been much better – the country newspapers had carried stories of struggles of shepherds in many places.

'You must have had a hard time up here,' I suggested.

'Yes,' replied the old shepherd. 'There wus times here, when I wus the miserablest man in all Gloucestershire. Sometimes I had nothing more dry to put on. During the whole of the lambing I wusn't gone from them more than two hours at a time.' Then, after a pause, he added: 'These young gentlemen, as comes to shepherding these days, thinks that to look to the flock once a week is enough. But I tell you, sheep, you know, are like children – they need a lot from you.'

'Yes, I'm sure they do,' I replied. Then I recounted what I had heard over the last weeks, about the wet, and the losses in the flocks – sixty lambs here, forty ewes there, thirty lambs somewhere else.

'Do you know,' he said, 'you'll hardly believe it, but I only lost three of 'em.' And then – standing there, on the top of that hill, in Easter week – he added a memorable thing: '*But then, of course, I loved 'em with me life!*'

It was easy, thereafter, to come down from that hill thinking of another Hill, another Shepherd, *Who loved us 'with His life!'*

With The Shepherd

Many of us were fortunate to live where from childhood up, sheep were familiar. Among the very first treasurable things we learned by heart, was the Twenty-third Psalm:

> The Lord is my shepherd; I shall not want.
> He maketh me to lie down in green pastures:
> He leadeth me beside the still waters.
> He restoreth my soul:
> He leadeth me in the paths of righteousness for his name's sake.
> Yea, though I walk through the valley of the shadow of death,
> I will fear no evil: for thou art with me;
> Thy rod and thy staff they comfort me.
> Thou preparest a table before me in the presence of mine enemies:
> Thou anointest my head with oil; my cup runneth over.
> Surely goodness and mercy shall follow me all the days of my life:
> And I will dwell in the house of the Lord for ever.

Anna Buchan – writer sister of John, Lord Tweedsmuir – told of the Thomson family. They came upon a sad day; and, gathered in the front room, their throats were tight with sorrow. Presently, their minister, the Reverend Mr Seaton, was shown in. He said immediately: 'We shall sing the Twenty-third Psalm.' *Sing?* The Thomsons looked at each other, and at their minister. But he well knew the healing to be had from this familiar thing – sung at weddings, at baptisms, and as fittingly when death darkened the doorway.

The Lord's my Shepherd, I'll not want.
He makes me down to lie
In pastures green: he leadeth me
The quiet waters by.

Yea, though I walk in Death's dark vale,
Yet will I fear none ill:
For thou art with me; and thy rod
And staff me comfort still.

One Summer, Rene, my home-making friend, and I took our haversacks and walked the Milford Track at the far south of our green land. Days and nights we spent with a small company, climbing and descending ways through immense forest, across rivers and streams, breathing mountain air. At night, we found lodging in solitary huts, set at agreed distances, and adequate in a simple way.

But one night, we wakened in the dark, to hear torrential rain hammering on our roof. And it hammered all that night, all the next day, and all the next night. A distant memory now was the golden sunshine in which we had set out. In no time, all the rivers were impassable, the smallest streams and waterfalls turbulent, the Track itself under water in many parts, the single connecting telephone line down. We were wholly cut off from the world, spending three nights there in Quinton Hut, instead of one.

Sunday found us still there, with nothing at all to remind us that it was Sunday. Mid-morning, someone moved to the old camp piano, and started to play a hymn. From a seat here and another there, people rose, until, about that old piano, a sing-song was in progress. In no time, there was a request for *The Lord's my Shepherd* to the loved tune 'Crimond'. But the tramper at the piano didn't know it, let alone that it drew its name from a little place in Aberdeenshire, and that our Queen, as a young bride, had chosen it for her wedding.

The only hymnbook, submerged amongst a pile of music, was no help. My friend, Rene, a long-time lover of 'Crimond', offered to play 'just this one', in her stead.

Instantly, to our surprise, the cookhouse door opened, and out stepped someone we'd never seen before, a rugged Track-man, driven in by the storm. Without a word, he took his place in that small circle and started to sing the tenor part, tune and word perfect. The instant it was over, he made his way back to where he had come from – and we never saw him again. 'Where,' we found ourselves asking silently, 'did he learn that loved Psalm – and what had it meant to him, in this isolated life?'

This is an immortal Psalm, loved by scholars and simple souls alike. In my student days, the latest Bible commentary was that much discussed volume by Professor Arthur Samuel Peake. 'Peake's great contribution,' a distinguished encourager dared to say, 'was that he brought to ordinary people a new view of the Bible, which liberated them from a narrow and rigid biblicism, and which did not offend, and left faith, not weaker, but stronger.' 'He took hold of the Twenty-third Psalm,' one of Peake's own students told us, 'and taught us what it meant, and he did more – *he never left us until we had seen the Shepherd.*'

I grew up needing what Peake's Commentary could do for me; and later, when I was able to journey in Palestine, I was able to follow and photograph an Eastern shepherd, such as is at the heart of this Psalm. One thing obvious to me, coming from a land of sheep, was that here the shepherd *led* his sheep, his flock being but a small one, whereas I was used to a shepherd who *drove* his sheep from behind, aided by docile, wise, well-trained dogs.

And the setting was so different: in the East were no spacious pastures as we know them, for in Palestine the shepherd had always to be moving his flock, seeking out patches of growing food. Being so few in number, their relationship was a very intimate one. Rihbany, a Syrian, tells of a shepherd named Yusuf, whom he knew in his boyhood. 'When I think,' he says, 'of that deep rocky gorge where Yusuf wintered his flock, and the many similar valleys which the shepherds have to traverse daily; when I think of the wild beasts they have to fight, and the scars they bear on their bodies as marks of their unreserved and boundless devotion to their flocks, I realize very clearly the depth of the Psalmist's faith.' The shepherd had constantly to be alert in these rocky defiles, and in scarce pastures, where vipers lurked to nip the noses of the sheep. And besides these, there were human robbers, as well as wolves. It was not uncommon for a sheep to fall into the bottom of a pit dug by a scheming robber and covered over with turf. The robber had to do that, or he could not claim what fell therein. (There is ample reference to this miserable device throughout Scripture; in Proverbs is a verse: 'Whoso causeth the upright to go astray in an evil way, he shall fall himself into his own pit' (28:10, AV). And again, in Psalm 7:15, is this warning: 'He hath made a pit and digged it, and is fallen into the ditch which he made. His mischief shall return upon his own head.' Another speaks of similar evil, in this wise: 'He brought me up out of an horrible pit' (Psalm 40:2, AV). The Psalmist is here using it as a word-picture of his spiritual experience. Recovery, he well knew, depended on the prompt, loving deliverance of the shepherd.

Then there was the tendency of a sheep *to wander*, seeking out fresh pastures for himself – only to lose his way altogether, or be caught within the briars. Again, deliverance depended on the caring qualities of the good shepherd. He who lacks this loving care is an hireling. Again and again there is tender reference to the lambs of the flock. Isaiah says, in a familiar passage: 'He shall gather the lambs in his arm and carry them in his bosom, and shall gently lead those that are with young' (40:11, AV). (A dog or cat can be relied upon to find its way home, when lost – but not a sheep.) Jesus, Who called Himself 'The Good Shepherd', well understood that He would have to do the seeking. Dr William Russell Maltby, treasuring this great reality, wrote sensitively:

> Where are You going, Shepherd?
> To find My sheep.
> How far will You go?
> As far as My sheep.
> How far may that be?
> To the world's end.
> How long will You seek it?
> Until I find it.
>
> When You find it, will it come to You?
> No, it will fly from Me.
> Where will it go then?
> To the rocks and the sand.
> When will it stop?
> When it can run no more.
> What will You do then?
> *Carry it home.*

There is meaning still, one finds, in the Psalmist's gracious words '*He leadeth me beside the still waters*'. This is acknowledgement of the need of refreshment and renewal. More than that, sheep will not drink of swirling, turbulent waters and the Shepherd knows that; he will find for us what we need, as we follow His lead. Though in this life one may fall, even into the equivalent of the deceptive pit, our Shepherd will hasten to restore His own to Himself, and from then on lead purposely forward in 'the path of His righteousness, for His name's sake'. In Biblical days, one's name was proof of one's character: one can trust the Good

Shepherd. His name and His nature are alike, utterly dependable, utterly loving.

This does not, of course, mean in any way that any one of us can bypass the Valley-of-the-Shadow. *It has to be traversed – but not alone!* Stephen Haboush, in looking back on *My Shepherd Life in Galilee* (published by Harper & Row) says 'I used to dread taking the sheep through one particular valley in Galilee. It is called the *Wadi el-nnar*. Next to the Dead Sea, it is the hottest place in Palestine, being over five hundred feet below sea-level. An ancient road runs through this valley . . . My sheep would sense the danger, *and gather closely to my side*. My continual calling, and the sense of my presence gave them confidence and allayed their fear.'

Stephen Haboush mentions for our comfort in this daily journey that we take, the rod and the staff that the shepherd used in Biblical days – which in small flocks nowadays have given way to the crook. These spelled assurance that a shepherd could deal with any situation.

Many, it appears, have taken the verse '*Thou preparest a table before me in the presence of mine enemies*', as unrelated to the simplicities of the remainder of the Psalm. This seems a pity.(All the scholars on whom I lean for direction, put in a plea for the retention of the pastoral image.) The shepherd story has not suddenly jumped to reference to a kingly spread. When we say of one whom we know, 'she keeps a good table', we mean, 'she serves a good meal'. And here, I feel, the reference is to a meal out under the wide sky – part of the shepherding life. Dr James Moffatt renders this reality: 'Thou art my host, spreading a feast for me, while my foes have to look on.' Another who firmly believes that the pastoral allegory is unbroken, is the Reverend James Neil, examining chaplain to the Bishop of Jerusalem and author of *Everyday Life in the Holy Land*. Both these men are steeped in Palestine's shepherd lore.

So we reach this little Psalm's happy ending: 'Surely

goodness and mercy shall follow me all the days of my life: and I shall dwell in the house of the Lord for ever.' The heart of religion lies in its personal pronouns. It carries a blithe confidence, based on personal experience. No wonder it wins its way into so many hearts: *we cannot do without this sublime picture of the Shepherd Who cares!*

Under The Stars

Only in the country can one now stand under the stars and see them as clearly as the Psalmist did. Neon lights spoil this experience for many of us who live in towns and cities. However rarely we feel this measure of our insignificance – even if only during holiday time in the country – it brings a kinship with the Psalmist. He says beautifully:

When I consider thy heavens, the work of thy fingers,
The moon and the stars, which thou hast ordained;
What is man, that thou art mindful of him?
And the son of man, that thou visitest him?
For thou hast made him a little lower than the angels,
And hast crowned him with glory and honour.
Thou madest him to have dominion over the works of thy hands;
Thou hast put all things under his feet:
All sheep and oxen,
Yea, and the beasts of the field;
The fowl of the air, and the fish of the sea,
And whatsoever passeth through the paths of the seas.
O Lord, our Lord,
How excellent is thy name in all the earth!
(Psalm 8:3–9, AV)

Two things stand out: *the greatness of God in His created world, and the insignificance of man in that world.* This is our dual experience still, out under the stars. More so, I dare think, than in the time of the Psalmist, although to him it was breathtaking. Modern scientists have opened up for us a vision unbelievably greater. Through a telescope, the stars are so many more, and so much greater to our thus aided eyes.

The Psalmist, marvelling, says: 'Thou hast put all things under his feet.' In our day, in a more literal sense, Sir Edmund Hillary – New Zealand bee-keeper turned mountaineer, and conqueror of Everest – said as if echoing the Psalmist: 'I had the world lie beneath my clumsy boots.' There is glory in that.

But the most lasting realization out under the stars is the *insignificance* of man. 'What is man,' the Psalmist found himself bound to exclaim, 'that thou art mindful of him? And the son of man, that thou visitest him?' This must have been the reaction, greatly multiplied, for Galileo, the first man ever to look at the stars above him through an instrument as powerful as he had. That was on the night of 7 January 1610. Immense progress has been made since, heightening that impact. Rupert Brooke in our century, with the facilities available to him, confessed that out-of-doors he felt 'like a fly crawling on the score of the Fifth Symphony'.

But size is not the criterion in this matter, as the Psalmist believed. God is not only great, but *gracious*. His character has been more fully revealed in the New Testament. This is of primary importance in the crisis of identity. When, under the stars, any one of us has an overwhelming sense of insignificance, he must accept that the matter does not turn on size. There are other values. Only his body is small, compounded of chemical constituents that can be measured and weighed. There is much more to man; there is his mind and his spirit. I like the way Thornton Wilder puts it in his well-known play *Our Town*. 'I don't care what they say with their mouths – everybody knows that *something* is eternal. And it ain't houses and it ain't names, and it ain't earth, *and it ain't even stars* – everybody knows in their bones that something is eternal, and *that* something has to do with human beings. All the greatest people who ever lived have been telling us that for five thousand years, and yet you'd be surprised how people are always losing hold of it. *There's something way down deep that's eternal about every human being.*'

In Roman days, and in those of ancient Greece, men, women and children were cheap, because values were awry. Aristotle is remembered to have said: 'Master and slave have nothing in common: a slave is a living tool, just as a tool is an inanimate slave.' And Varo as damningly stated his judgement, when, in his treatise on the Romans, he divided the means of agriculture into 'the articulate, comprising the slaves, the inarticulate, comprising the cattle, and the mute, comprising the vehicles'. Men were but things to be exchanged for money.

'What is man?' is the Psalmist's question. And I am bound to echo: 'What am I?' but the answer does not depend on size, on one's feeling out under the stars, or on one's estimate at another time, like that of Rupert Brooke. It depends on God's summing up; and He has made us all 'a little lower than the angels, crowned with glory and honour'. Dr Leslie Weatherhead, in *The Christian Agnostic*, puts it well: 'Part of our difficulty,' he says, 'in this problem of God's providence is that we cannot escape *anthropomorphism* – thinking of God as a big man. Many cannot really believe in their hearts that God can be concerned in the troubles of *an insignificant individual* on one of the minor planets which itself is only a speck of cosmic dust in an immense universe the size of which no brain can really conceive.'

A certain awed humility which some interpreters see in this question of the Psalmist, is well enough. But where it becomes a disabling sense of insignificance, as it does for many, it is an unworthy reference to God, Whom we know *not only as Creator and Provider*, but as *Father*. Our Lord taught us to call Him this. His most widely-known parable, that of the Prodigal Son, shows a person to be precious, and his homecoming welcomed with glory and love. To this Jesus added a further group of stories, lest one should find it hard to believe so much, when one feels so small. He spoke not only of 'the one son', but also of 'the one sheep', 'the one coin'. He talked of 'the fifth sparrow' in Matthew 10:29: 'Are not *two* sparrows sold for a farthing?' – and again, in Luke 12:6: 'Are not *five* sparrows sold for two farthings, *and not one of them is forgotten before God*?' Such – even the little odd, seemingly worthless sparrow thrown into the bargain for nothing, when the larger deal could be made, 'two for one farthing, five for two' – was not unvalued. And our Lord went on to use His 'how much more' argument. The least human being, He stressed, is of infinite worth. Even drop-outs from school, college and society as we know them, count in His reckoning. Someone who under the stars is insignificant, is nevertheless loved of God, redeemed by Christ the Saviour, and destined in the everlasting purpose for Immortality.

To those of us who delight in this reality, Wordsworth's words walk up and down in the mind:

> Whether we be young or old,
> Our destiny, our being's heart and home,
> Is with infinitude, and only there;
> With hope it is, hope that can never die;
> Effort and expectation and desire,
> And something evermore about to be!

On My Way

The joy of the pilgrim heart is treasurable. And the Psalmist knew it when he sang:

> How amiable are thy tabernacles,
> O Lord of hosts!
> My soul longeth, yea, even fainteth for the courts
>   of the Lord:
> My heart and my flesh crieth out for the living God.
> Yea, the sparrow hath found an house,
> And the swallow a nest for herself, where she may lay her
>   young,
> Even thine altars, O Lord of hosts,
> My King, and my God.
> Blessed are they that dwell in thy house:
> They will be still praising thee.
> Blessed is the man whose strength is in thee;
> In whose heart are the ways of them.
>
> (Psalm 84:1–5, AV)

But Dr James Moffatt makes these last lines more graphic; in the Authorized Version they are rather colourless. I am grateful to Dr Moffatt, and he translates the original Hebrew of the Psalmist's words: '*Happy are they who, nerved by thee, set out on pilgrimage!*' (v.5). It is so full of joy and vitality! We men and women of these days of speedy travel, know little of the anticipation and the satisfaction of the pilgrim Psalmist, and those who accompanied him.

In those days, the roads and the hazards of travel were such that men and women leaving for any distant place, knew it was wise to set out together. They could then know not only joyous company, but physical safety; the roads stretching afar were all too often hiding places for brigands. When the goal was a spiritual sharing – as in the experience of those who journeyed on foot to worship in Jerusalem – much was added by going together.

Others, in other times, were as happy as the Psalmist to express themselves in his words: 'Happy are they who, nerved by thee, set out on pilgrimage!' Others soon caught the joy of this song.

One can imagine the thoroughness of preparation, for such a pilgrimage was often an experience of a lifetime. A pilgrimage on foot meant that sandals had to be checked, and there were certain other needs of the way – travelling, eating, sleeping needs – that had to be catered for. The time of starting had to be settled, and companions met. No wonder excitement mounted as the day drew near.

It was only when I was myself in Palestine, with some chance to measure many distances travelled on foot by pilgrims – distances that, even travelling by car, tired me in the heat – that I gathered any idea of what it once meant. And the Psalmist's words marched up and down in my mind, with new meaning. The larger the company, I suspect, the slower the travelling; and sometimes there would be old folk, women and children, at least of twelve years old, as was Jesus when He went up to Jerusalem on His first pilgrimage. That involved a lot. It was Springtime, the great pilgrimage time of the Passover. Many people were on the roads. Even family donkeys – saddles and traces adjusted – must have sensed the air of widespread excitement. As the company pressed on, there was the joy of mingling with other caravans, in fellowship and expectation. Along with them, were several families they knew.

For Joseph and Mary's boy, it was the first time He had ever been beyond the limitations of little Nazareth. Doubtless, He had often wondered what lay beyond those familiar hills, on the road leading out. A new world awaited Him there each time they breasted a hilltop. Beauty was everywhere – across the rich plain Spring grasses were green, flowers opening dewy faces in the sun, birds busy with their nest-building. Up and down, the group followed the leader – past sprouting corn patches, and occasional shady, blue-green olive groves. A joyful company they were, from time to time singing the songs of their people, rich, ancient songs, to the music of the flute:

> I was glad when they said unto me
> 'Let us go into the House of the Lord!'
> Our feet shall stand within Thy gates,
> O Jerusalem!

Who can know with what dreams that one lad lay down to sleep on the simple, improvised bed, made from what they'd brought from home? But at last, dawn saw them astir once more. Jesus knew that He would soon see the Holy City for Himself.

Footsore and dusty they were, but how little that mattered! Their prayers and Songs of Ascent rose higher. That sundown, they pitched camp on the Mount of Olives. Just across the ravine of Kedron, no distance, were at last the gleaming outlines of the Temple, quarried from white stone, and roofed in part with gold.

Next morning, wakened by 'the bright stridency of the silver trumpets blown at the sun's up-rising', they finished their pilgrimage. There were shocks, as well as delights: the lowing of frightened cattle for sacrifice, the bleating of sheep and goats, the distress cries of hapless doves and pigeons beside the slaughter-house. Excluding notices shocked Jesus, too: 'Let no foreigner enter within the screen and enclosure around the Holy Place. Whosoever is taken so doing will himself be the cause that death overtakes him.' Could the prophet Isaiah have spoken wrongly when he told of the Temple as the *House of Prayer for all nations*? And there were the money-changers – greedily gloating over their coins. But there was worship; there was singing; and the glories of Feast-time passed all too soon. An experience never to be forgotten!

The passing days might dim the sharp edges of that pilgrimage for some – but not for one lad. Nor was He likely to forget the hour His parents sought Him out and found Him in the Temple, together with the doctors of the Law. It was all part of the total pilgrimage – and soon He was on His way homeward. He had learned that things both painful and perplexing can happen to a pilgrim. The way is sometimes uphill, night comes chill about him, whereas by day the sun beats mercilessly down. And there can be dangers unguessed before home is reached.

When, nearer our own time, Chaucer led his pilgrims down through the English countryside, to Canterbury-towne, he did not forget the hazards; and an old manuscript, penned shortly after Chaucer's death, provides against unhappy elements in the undertaking. 'I say to thee,' it begins, 'that it is well done that Pilgrims have with them singers and also pipers, and that when one of them that goeth bare-foot striketh his toe upon a stone, and hurteth it sore, and maketh him to bleed, it is well done that he or his fellow begin then a song, or else take out of his bosom a pipe to drive away with such mirth the hurt of his fellow.'

Sometimes a pilgrimage is not a matter of geography but rather a good purpose of the spirit, in good company, to a good end. And in either sense we may lay hold of the Psalmist's words: '*Happy are they who, nerved by thee, set out on pilgrimage!*' Here and now, we may, any one of us, walk with a shining light in our eyes. For we are not spiritual tramps – we are pilgrims. And there is a world of difference! Margot Asquith took pains, in her autobiography, to make this known and understood. In the English-Scottish Border country that she knew so well, she talked to many a man of the road, knowing no fear or suspicion. To one old fellow she dared to say: 'You seem to walk all day and go nowhere.' And indeed, that was true. 'When you wake up in the morning,' asked she, 'how do you shape your course?' And when he gave her his answer, she knew she was talking to a tramp and not to a pilgrim, for he answered her question: 'I always turn my back to the wind.' That settled the matter. *For a tramp is on the way to nowhere in particular, seeking only an easy way; but a pilgrim has an on-going way to a certain chosen goal out of sight.*

In the realm of the Spirit, you and I are called to be pilgrims, lest loving this world as we do, with its companionship and delightful purposes, we forget why we are here, and what our goal is at last. 'Happy are they who, nerved by thee, set out on pilgrimage!' Wonderful!

Singing With The Psalmists

The best that we can say of the Psalmists is that they were *aware*. When they experienced ordinary day-to-day happenings; or life moved them to the cry of despair, the wail of sorrow; or uncovered before their God the soul's deep longing; or allowed them the moving wonder of exultation – their words did not echo from a void, but awakened in them loving and wondering praise, to the glory of God the Eternal.

At one time, men and women in our time imagined that all the Psalms were the utterance of one person: David, the shepherd-boy, later King. What they read were referred to as 'The Psalms of David'. But that was too easy an answer. Undoubtedly some of the Psalms were first sung by David; but the Psalm heading 'Of David' doesn't necessarily mean 'By David'. Dr Theodore H. Robinson has underlined this for us most helpfully. We see other singers – recognizing sayings reminiscent of David (as recorded in the book of Samuel) – adding the headings as suitable, a tribute. 'It is now,' says Dr Robinson, 'more generally held that the names set above the Psalms indicate collections from which the Psalms were taken – just as the term "Sankey's Hymns" is often applied to a number of hymns which were not written by Ira D. Sankey, though they were included in the collections which bear his name.'

Another point to remember, if we are to enter into the mood of the Psalms, is the extraneous religious thought that is often incorporated; the Hebrews were not the only people who sang songs. There were pagan peoples all about them, and they had their influence. Some knowledge of historical events of those times is a help in accounting for much that might otherwise raise questions in our minds. Many parts of the Psalms are savage and revengeful. We can skip such passages – but we are bound to admit that they exist.

Professor Oesterley, another modern scholar, with knowledge of Hebrew songs, says: 'The periods during which the Psalms were written cover many centuries; therefore the religious conceptions set forth in them necessarily differ greatly in spirit and in content.' He does not skip the savage and unlovely sections that we would never teach our children, as we teach them Psalm 23 and some others, which we use together in our church worship, or one by one in our private devotions. Psalm 137, for instance, expresses dreadful sentiments: 'O daughter of Babylon' could as fittingly be introduced in our day as 'O daughter of Dachau', or some other Nazi concentration camp; 'Happy shall he be that taketh and dasheth thy little ones against the stones.' We modern users of these ancient songs cannot repeat such vengeful cries, but their existence helps us to be realistic, and to know what lies in the heart of man unredeemed.

We are on safe ground when we recognize that *the Psalms were sung by many different singers, out of varying experiences, over a long period of time*. The lasting wonder is that many of them rose to rare heights of beauty, strength and devotion. These enrich our lives – breathing for us, in their own particular type of poetry, the delight of the earth, the stars, the seas, and all-beholding sun; the cry of the fugitive hunted for his life; the heart of the righteous smitten and afflicted, the deep secret pangs of remorse, humiliation and repentance; and the wonderful reality of forgiveness; with stirring songs of citizenship, joys of pilgrimage, and good hospitality received and offered. And all these things are seen as part of a progressive revelation. There is nowhere in all literature such a cross-section of human living, in so small a space. A hundred and fifty songs, they are divided in our collection into five short books:

I. Psalms 1–41
II. Psalms 42–72
III. Psalms 73–89
IV. Psalms 90–106
V. Psalms 107–150.

Much of the Old Testament can be described as 'the words of man addressed to man', other parts as 'the words of God addressed to man', but here in the Psalms, to a degree not found anywhere else, are 'the words of man addressed to God'.

Dr Hermann Gunkel, in publishing his studies, did much to help us present-day readers of the Psalms. To what other scholars had offered, he added comments on the various types of Psalms: hymns, laments, thanksgivings, royal psalms, wisdom psalms, pilgrim songs, and minor songs. Some contain elements of more than one type. And the wonder of God's creative and providential care, in Nature, recurs. Thus –

> He causeth the grass to grow for the cattle,
> And herb for the service of man:
> That he may bring forth food out of the earth;
> And wine that maketh glad the heart of man,
> And oil to make his face to shine,
> And bread which strengtheneth man's heart.
> (104:14–15, AV)

And the lesser creatures are remembered as well:

> The trees of the Lord are full of sap;
> The cedars of Lebanon, which he hath planted;

Where the birds make their nests:
As for the stork, the fir trees are her house.
The high hills are a refuge for the wild goats;
And the rocks for the conies.

(104:16–18, AV)

Another Psalmist rejoices in the provision for the sparrow, of common, constant attendance; and for the swallow, a migratory bird, of casual appearance. So we are told of the sparrow's house and the swallow's nest:

How amiable are thy tabernacles,
 O Lord of hosts!
My soul longeth, yea, even fainteth
 for the courts of the Lord;
My heart and my flesh crieth out for the living God.

Yea, the sparrow hath found an house,
And the swallow a nest for herself,
 where she may lay her young,
Even thine altars, O Lord of hosts,
My King, and my God.

(84:1–3, AV)

We each have a favourite Psalm, or a handful of favourites. As a child, I earned an occasional sixpence for learning a fresh one, and reciting it without faltering. Dr Mary Ellen Chase, of Smith College – author of *The Psalms for the Common Reader* (W. W. Norton & Company Inc., New York) – knew a similar source of childish income, and learned the 23rd, the 19th, the 121st, and the 100th, among others. 'At home,' said she, 'my father, with the help of Psalm 91, aptly characterized a great-aunt of ours, whom none of us much liked. When we heard that she was coming for dinner with us, he defined her as "the destruction that wasteth at noonday"; and whenever she stayed for the night, she became "the pestilence that walketh in darkness". Although my mother,' added Dr Chase, 'was given to reproaching him for his employment of such holy words, we children delighted in them.'

But, even knowing all this, before we can set forth into discovery in the Psalms, we must know that a characteristic of Hebrew poetry is what the scholars have taught us to call *parallelism*. In its first, and simplest, form, a second sentence is made to repeat the first:

> The king sent and loosed him,
> The ruler of the people let him go free.

In a second form the second sentence serves an opposite truth:

> The Lord knoweth the way of the righteous,
> But the way of the ungodly shall perish.

In a third form, the second sentence completes the first by giving some consequence of the first:

> But now shall my head be lifted up
> Above my enemies round about me.

Dr Robert Lowth, an English scholar and lover of the Psalms, designated each of these forms in which parallelism was the framework: synonymous, antithetic, and synthetic. (If one forgets these titles, the three forms are plain enough.) And there is another that he called climactic – stair-like, step-by-step, or wave-after-wave:

Give unto the Lord, O ye mighty,
Give unto the Lord, glory and strength,
Give unto the Lord, the glory due unto his name.

So these songs depend not on metre or rhyme, as we are accustomed to in our English poetry, but on a balance of thought. Then an ingenious acrostic structure is used, starting with the first letter of the Hebrew alphabet, and going on down through its twenty-two letters (as in Psalms 111 and 112). In another instance each two-line stanza gives way to a change of letter (as in Psalm 34). In another (as in the long Psalm 119), the pattern is expanded on a use of eight verses. Each of the first eight begins with *Aleph*, and so on to the end. One greatly daring translator attempted to preserve this form for us in English – but the outcome was disastrous. He managed well enough with 'A'; and even 'B' wasn't too awkward:

By what means must a young man cleanse his way?
  Thy word must e'en his canon be,
Betimes I heartily thy presence sought,
  Nor thy command could errant flee.
Because thy words are hid within my heart
  I shall not give offence to thee.

A little wooden, I fear, and unmusical, as it proceeds. But by the letter 'N' he was in real trouble; and when he had to face 'O', and later 'Q', the result, far from being devotional, was ludicrous:

Querked, I gasped for breath, and sweet relief
  in thy commandment comes at last.
Quemeful and kindly, turn thy face on me
  as aye on them that love thee well.
Queachy my foothold . . .

But enough – more than enough – we are in a bog, and it sounds like it!

* * *

In the discoveries I have made in the Psalms, the word *delight* occurs again and again. It seems unlikely that wherever the word is upon the lips, we are indebted to one and the same Psalmist. (I find it in Psalm 1 verse 2; in Psalm 16:3; in Psalm 37:4; again in Psalm 51:15 and 16, all of that loved modern version, the Revised Standard Version. And there may be others I have not yet discovered.) Sufficient to claim that the Psalmists who take their singing seriously, do not feel moved to take it always solemnly.

I like best what they say in the familiar Authorized Version, moving on to the Revised Standard Version, with occasional excursions into the version of Dr Moffatt. These walk up and down in my mind, bringing new understanding of life, and with delight, sing in my heart.

Called To Worship

The Psalms, we soon discover as we adventure into them, centre round the conception of a monotheistic God – the *One and Only God.* This is much more remarkable than it first strikes us to be, for the nations surrounding most of those who fashioned the Psalms were worshippers of gods many and varied. Some of those gods were cruel, immoral and unpredictable. Those who worshipped the One God – holy, merciful, and provident – were at a great advantage. Not least for this reason did the words with which what is now Psalm 29 opened, find an immediate response in human hearts:

> Give unto the Lord the glory due unto his name;
> *Worship the Lord in the beauty of holiness.*
>
> (AV)

Many to whom these words were addressed were familiar with 'the voice of the Lord' in Nature. Seven times in this brief Psalm, mention is made of 'the voice of the Lord'.

> Give unto the Lord, O ye mighty,
> Give unto the Lord glory and strength.
> Give unto the Lord the glory due unto his name;
> Worship the Lord in the beauty of holiness.
> The voice of the Lord is upon the waters:
> The God of glory thundereth:
> The Lord is upon many waters.
> The voice of the Lord is powerful;
> The voice of the Lord is full of majesty.
> The voice of the Lord breaketh the cedars:
> Yea, the Lord breaketh the cedars of Lebanon.
> He maketh them also to skip like a calf;

Lebanon and Sirion like a young unicorn.
The voice of the Lord divideth the flames of fire.
The voice of the Lord shaketh the wilderness;
The Lord shaketh the wilderness of Kadesh.
The voice of the Lord maketh the hinds to calve,
And discovereth the forests:
And in his temple doth every one speak of his glory.
The Lord sitteth upon the flood;
Yea, the Lord sitteth King for ever.
The Lord will give strength unto his people;
The Lord will bless his people with peace.

Stars overhead, and lands spread out, were the creation of the God Whom they worshipped; the sun that ruled their comings and goings by day, was His, as was the moon, that calmly beamed down in the time of their rest. All around, when their eyes and hearts were responsive, were countless forms of Nature, and all to God's glory!

And ever since, wherever we men and women live, it has continued to be so. No wonder St Benedict was led to exclaim: 'Nothing must precede the worship of God!' The world of Nature that we look upon is very different from that known to the Psalmists, and those then called to worship; but it is still the creation of God. Those in our midst who have come to be known as our great naturalists have not all found their way easily to Him. For many years of his life Richard Jefferies refused to recognize the Creator, calling himself atheist. But there came a time when, in sickness, towards the end of his days, he completely changed his approach, and to his wife said: 'I have done wrong, and thought wrong; it was my intellectual vanity.'

In all our modern-day hymnbooks there is space for the worship of God through Nature, added to the words of the Psalmists, to some of which I have delighted to draw attention; and in that respect I may eagerly include Psalm 19, among others:

> The heavens declare the glory of God;
>   And the firmament sheweth his handywork.
> Day unto day uttereth speech,
>   And night unto night sheweth knowledge.
> There is no speech nor language,
>   Where their voice is not heard.

One of our most used hymns begins:

> O worship the King,
>   All glorious above;
> O gratefully sing
>   His power and his love . . .

and it goes on referring to Creation in verse after verse:

> O tell of his might,
>   O sing of his grace,
> Whose robe is the light,
>   Whose canopy space;
> His chariots of wrath
>   The deep thunder-clouds form,
> And dark is his path
>   On the wings of the storm.

> The earth with its store
>   Of wonders untold,
> Almighty! Thy power
>   Hath founded of old,

Hath stablished it fast
  By a changeless decree,
And round it hath cast
  Like a mantle, the sea.

Thy bountiful care
  What tongue can recite?
It breathes in the air,
  It shines in the light,
It streams from the hills,
  It descends to the plain,
And sweetly distils
  In the dew and the rain . . .

This accompanies the mood of the Psalmist – in worship, glorifying the God of Nature. And where Nature smiles, it is easy to sing like this. St Francis found it so, in Assisi. His superb hymn has a place in most of our modern hymnbooks:

All creatures of our God and King,
Lift up your voice, and with us sing:
  Alleluia! Alleluia!

Looking at the white oxen of Assisi drawing home their great wooden harvest-wagons, I found myself singing it.

And I worshipped God, and glorified His name, just as easily one Spring tramping in England. Pack on back, with my friend I came one morning to the tiny Cornish church of St Enodoc. Early on, the hedges by the way were gleaming with dew, now the breeze was dipping into them. Over a stile that gave entrance to a sward of green, a path led on until we came to the church. It was one of the loveliest finds, and one of the simplest. The sweet sea air gave us blessing, along with the warmth of the sun overhead. The tiny church, we learned, had at one time been buried in the sands that blew in; and it had stayed that way, hidden, for two hundred years. No one could open its door. But once a year, an aperture made in the roof allowed a clergyman to be let through to conduct worship, to maintain the privileges of the church. Imagine it! There, within sound of the distant breakers, larks overhead provided Nature's music. Over the daisy-dappled grass beyond the mown path we trod, the spire of the restored building greeted us, having been dug out of the piled sands by modern tools. And all about it was peace, broken only by the voices of a little knot of children. They fell silent as we drew near to ask why the organ was being played. They told us that it was nearly time for Sunday School. Soon they were gathered in, and we took our leave. The last thing we heard from them (and shall we ever forget it?) was their thin, sweet voices singing their opening hymn:

> We love the place, O God,
> Wherein thine honour dwells . . .

They were not Psalmists, nor children of Psalmists; nor could they know much of the Psalmists' background – but they in turn were learning to worship. And there is nothing like it. 'Worship,' wrote Evelyn Underhill, in her classic of that title, 'is the response of the creature to the Eternal.' It is a mood of reverent acknowledgement, of thanksgiving, awe, joy, and adoring praise. And company, occasion and architecture can help it. Pearson hoped that his cathedral in Truro would 'bring a man to his knees'. 'To worship,' said Dr William Temple, 'is to quicken the conscience by the holiness of God, to feed the mind with the truth of God, to purge the imagination by the beauty of God, to open the heart to the love of God, and to devote the will to the purpose of God.' The Psalmists would have understood that, though I can't find them anywhere actually proffering definitions. For all that, I love those words of Dr William Temple's better than many: *deeds are worth more, in the sight of God, than definitions.*

Every part of our worship service should be planned to serve this supreme end, with awe and wonder foremost. Faith matters much, issuing in adoration, penitence, an acceptance of forgiveness (and a readiness to give it), thanksgiving, intercession and dedication.

'Has worship relevance for these modern times?' was a question put to me lately by one who asked what I was writing. I told her about this book on the Psalms; but there was no time, at the entrance of the Food Market, to tell her what I was delighting in. I realized that her question was asked in all seriousness.

For we have much in common with the Psalmist. It is the fault of every modern age that it attempts to cut itself off from earlier ages by claiming some vast difference between them. It is true, of course, that the setting is different in many ways; but there is, wherever we live, a continuing human condition that at heart makes us kin to the Psalmist. The relevance of worship is real, because it's a question of our relationship, one by one, with God – and with our fellows. Forms and orders and times of that worship are, to some degree, secondary. The great thing is that we know that worship is not something which the Church through the centuries has agreed to take over from the Old Testament Temple services; it is the matching of a basic human need, set within our threefold being of body, mind and spirit. When we worship, we one by one recognize this, as being always relevant. Our Master Jesus, as man, attended the synagogue, and taught in the Temple – and on one occasion even took a lash of small cords to the greedy money-changers set to make profit there. And when asked by His close followers to teach them to pray, He did so. We have the very prayer He taught, incorporated in our worship. Nothing in our life matters more than what we do on the first day of the week as part of a congregation, and, more frequently, on our own in private. It puts all interests, plans and comings and goings, all values and human relationships in the family and community, into proper perspective.

From the beginning, this was recognized by the early Christians, and became one of their most distinguishing characteristics. Pliny the Younger, as early as AD 61–113, wrote officially as Governor of Bithynia, to ask Emperor Trajan what he should do with the Christians – charge them with being Christians, or leave them alone? He tells of their worship: 'As their custom was, they assembled on a fixed day before daybreak, shared a hymn to Christ as a god, and together took an oath (*sacramentum*) . . . and these things done, strengthened in fellowship, dispersed to their ordinary concerns.' But for that 'custom' – always, in the Roman Empire, a dangerous one – we should not today find ourselves inheritors of this experience of reality.

A hundred and fifty years ago in Scotland, so Dr George MacLeod informs us, a man could be arrested and brought before a civil magistrate for neglecting to assure that *his wife* went to worship on Sunday morning. It was a situation on which a modern rhymster felt he ought to have something to say:

> Take my wife and let her be
> Consecrated, Lord, to thee.
> Help her now thy will to see,
> But please, dear Lord, don't count on me.

That man missed much. He fell short of the Psalmist of many centuries ago, and of the brave early Christians.

Skipping From My Tongue

Many of us still discover delight in memorizing Bible passages. Molly Weir tells of this discovery early in her life, in *Best Foot Forward*: 'I fell under the spell of the Bible.' She related then how she would 'race along to school chanting: "Tell it not in Gath, publish it not in the streets of Askelon, lest the daughters of the Philistines rejoice, lest the daughters of the uncircumcised triumph." And as I turned the corner,' she added, 'I wailed: "Ye daughters of Israel weep over Saul, who clothed you in scarlet and other delights, who put ornaments of gold upon your apparel." What marvellous sounds they were!'

Yes! Though I can't think, at that stage, that she knew much of what those words were about, only that they had a lively sound, and skipped from her tongue.

There are many passages in the Bible that offer the same fascination, as one speaks them, and many such passages are in the Psalms. There are, I have to admit, confusing passages, and some quite out of my depth; but there are others peculiarly 'my own', as Molly Weir found those she has quoted. One of my favourites – and being of some length, it took me a long while to learn – I finished on my earliest air flight overseas:

> O Lord, thou hast searched me, and known me.
> Thou knowest my downsitting and mine uprising,
>   Thou understandest my thought afar off.
> Though compassest my path and my lying down,
>   And art acquainted with all my ways.
> For there is not a word in my tongue,
>   But, lo, O Lord, thou knowest it altogether.

Thou hast beset me behind and before,
  And laid thine hand upon me.
Such knowledge is too wonderful for me;
  It is high, I cannot attain unto it.
Whither shall I go from thy spirit?
  Or whither shall I flee from thy presence?
If I ascend up into heaven, thou art there:
  If I make my bed in hell, behold, thou art there.
If I take the wings of the morning,
  And dwell in the uttermost parts of the sea;
Even there shall thy hand lead me,
  And thy right hand shall hold me.
If I say, Surely the darkness shall cover me;
  Even the night shall be light about me.
Yea, the darkness hideth not from thee;
  But the night shineth as the day:
The darkness and the light are both alike to thee!
(Psalm 139:1–12, AV)

I was delighted to find Dr Perowne saying: 'Nowhere are the attributes of God – His Omniscience, His Omnipotence, His Omnipresence – set forth so strikingly.' It confirmed my wisdom in having chosen this passage to lodge in my memory and repeat often, especially when alone out-of-doors. It came to mean more and more to me; and even now it may be that I have much still to discover of its total meaning. Perhaps I shall never wholly embrace all of it, whilst here in this life on earth. But it seems to offer great height and breadth and dignity. And as my mouth frames its words I feel sure that I am not alone, however removed from human company. I look at the world of Nature about me – its goodness, and greatness and majesty – and go over the words of my favourite Psalm again.

It comes easily to my mind as I set off on some plane trip, and find myself settled expectantly in my seat, with my future in glad eagerness. Some of my loveliest discoveries in life have come on such trips. Taking off, with mighty, revving engines, towns, cities, continents have taken on a new perspective. Soon, rivers have run as silver threads, lakes become burnished mirrors, mountains risen majestically, jungles seemed as mere parsley beds.

And never shall I forget the velvety darkness giving way to dawn, as when I flew into the Holy Land, with Mount Hermon's snowy form pushing up soon through a mantle of mist. I was in the mood to say over beneath my breath:

> O Lord, thou hast searched me, and known me.
> Thou knowest my downsitting and mine uprising . . .
> Thou hast beset me behind and before,
> And laid thine hand upon me . . .
> If I take the wings of the morning,
> And dwell in the uttermost parts of the sea;
> Even there shall thy hand lead me,
> And thy right hand shall hold me . . .

A little while ago, taking off from Denmark, where I had never been before – but where I found as surely the Omniscience, the Omnipotence and the Omnipresence of God – I was delighted to fly over 'Greenland's Icy Mountains', which for a moment brought to the forefront of memory an old missionary hymn familiar in my growing-up days, but one which I never hear today. I crossed over to the plane window to take a photograph but, flying so high, although everything beneath was excitingly, gently blue, I feared that my one effort might be wasted, and so took five pictures. Imagine my delight when all five were as telling, as clear as I could have desired. (Yet I don't need five good pictures, one is enough – and I scarcely need that to remind me of that experience.)

My sky-way took me on over mighty, spreading Canada where I had been on two former occasions, then travelling by train and car overland. Next the plane took me again to the States – over vast patterns of countryside spread widely, quiet and beautiful, however voluble and money-governed many things in that vast country might be on the ground. And at night even those cities held delight, as displays of jewellers' bracelets.

Some passengers, I know, find no such experience in air travel – indeed, A. P. Herbert, cheerful writer-politician and Englishman, declares it a bore. 'Of all the miracles of human might,' he says, 'the most fatiguing, I think, is flight. "It would be fine," we said, "for men to soar"; but now that we can do it, it's a bore.'

I can't agree. To me it is an experience of a fascinating dimension, full of beauty; and to one already aware of the Omniscience, Omnipotence and Omnipresence of God, a spiritual experience. But a great deal, of course, depends on what one brings to this experience. I am grateful that early in my time of growing up, I stowed away in my memory that great passage from the longest Psalm in the collection that has come down to us, whilst we have been learning to move further and further about God's world.

When last in England, I made an opportunity to visit the Commonwealth Air Force Memorial, on the hill above Runnymede, where history has left its mark so unforgettably. I was moved, in this more recent earthly area of human remembrance, to find awaiting me a rendering of my Psalm:

> If I climb up into Heaven, Thou art there;
> If I go down to Hell, Thou art there also.
> If I take the wings of the morning, and remain in the uttermost parts of the sea:
> Even there also shall Thy hand lead me;
> And Thy right hand shall hold me!

Wherever one finds oneself in this wonderful world – facing

whatever experiences of life or death, which come, as they do, to us all – it is worth having such words deeply implanted in the memory.

For some it is no longer the custom to learn things off by heart. I think this is a pity. Some unchanging truth is easily dropped like a seed into the human memory, and the earlier the better. There it grows to size and lovely strength, and life is ever afterwards richer.

With The Morning

Have you ever risen in the early dark, and gone to some nearby hilltop to see a new morning come, as I have several times on birthdays? You will know it as an exciting thing to do – and not only on a birthday. I felt an instant kinship with the man who wrote of his early morning experience on Tiger Hill, Darjeeling. 'This is a modest promontory,' said he to me, who had never myself been quite so near to the Himalayas, 'though to reach it seems a stiff climb in the small hours. From its summit one may command a view unsurpassed . . . The central feature of the kaleidoscope of colour that fills the valley and finally irradiates the tip of Everest!

'It is best seen from Tiger Hill, and around the crest is a fortress wall. To gain the summit one enters through the barrier. The charge? Two annas – but the enterprising and genial occupier increases this initial tuppence with the tea and sweet cakes familiar to all who have heard the cry of the char wallah in the land. But neither he nor his wall can hold out the sunrise. It fills the valleys and climbs mountains in a profusion of colours set to the music of the dawn chorus. It is reality once more, the miracle of every morning, *no less than the heavens declaring the glory of God.*'

One can be kin to the Psalmist – not only in his quotation, but in the fuller statement with which I took hold of this morning:

Give ear to my words, O Lord,
  Consider my meditation.
Hearken unto the voice of my cry, my King, and my God,
  For unto thee will I pray.

With The Morning

My voice shalt thou hear in the morning, O Lord;
In the morning will I direct my prayer unto thee, and will look up.

(Psalm 5:1–3, AV)

Scholars tell us that we have in this a hymn for morning sacrifice in the Temple, sharply personal in tone. While its references are related to the natural acts of the worship of the writer's time, its phrases are such that they can be applied to Christian worship in its most spiritual aspects. It is a Psalm from which the interpreter may take an image here, or a phrase there, and put himself in their charge, their true context being his own religious experience, or need, and that of the people whom he is addressing.

'The structure is evident. Verses 1–3 are a true "invocation". Verses 4–7 remind us that only those who seek harmony with the Divine Will can bring an offering of worship that will be acceptable, and particularly that the offering of the "man of blood" who has cruelty and hate in his heart, will be rejected. On the other hand, the worshipper's better state of mind is marked by awareness of God's mercy, through which alone he is permitted to enter the place of prayer, and by subsequent reverence; it is implied that thereby he may hope that his worship will be acceptable. Verses 8–12 are a prayer for divine light and leading in the difficulties created by men who wilfully misrepresent him . . . The conclusion is a strong instance of that complete confidence in God's ultimate vindication of the good, which like a trumpet melody runs through the varied music of the Psalms' (*The Interpreter's Bible*, Abingdon and Collins).

Every word in this morning utterance of the Psalmist is full of significance for us. We live in a different age; we worship in a different way; we may even be far from any appointed place of worship; we may be solitary in experience where the day finds us. But we have needs common to the Psalmist as a person long ago, and to countless individuals to this day. Nationality or sex has nothing to do with it. We are all dealing with the same God, unchanged by the centuries – save that He reveals Himself to us through Christ, more fully than ever. Added to the accumulated worship and service, and love to Him as the Eternal One, Whom the Psalmist speaks of as 'not a God Who delights in wickedness' (verse 4, RSV), Jesus, in the on-going, New Testament era, taught men and women to call God 'Our Father'. And this makes a great difference to our prayer still, in the early morning, as we waken to a new day. Clause by clause, ever since, men and women have greeted the morning with that loved term of address, and in all the languages in which they pray. No other prayer, as the morning comes, or at any other time, has such a hold upon the human heart, in corporate worship or in private prayer. So we are each richer by far than the Psalmist.

Jesus was not the first to address God as 'Father'. In Babylonia, in Egypt, in Greece, and in Rome, that gracious name was already known. 'O vast and distant Heaven who may be called our Father,' was the language of a Chinese ode more ancient than Confucius himself. 'Be easy of access to us, as a father to his sons,' ran the first hymn of *Rig-Veda*, the most ancient sacred literature of India. In the third century before Jesus Himself, the great stoic philosopher Cleanthes dared to pray: 'Draw men out from the gloom of their ignorance, scatter the darkness of their souls, O Father.'

Though Jesus never claimed to have invented that loved term of address, 'Our Father', He did imbue it with new content; He did bring it from the circumference of men's thinking, to the pivotal centre, especially in prayer. It was early upon His lips: 'Wist ye not,' we find Him saying to His distressed parents, Mary and Joseph, when they came upon Him as a lad of twelve in the Temple, 'that I must be about

My Father's business?' And His last, expiring utterance is even more impressive: '*Father*, into Thy hands, I commend My spirit!'

And at whatever hour we take these words upon our lips – especially in the morning, I think, when the whole day of human contacts lies ahead of one – they have expanded meaning. For to pray 'Our Father in Heaven', implies 'Our brother on earth'. This is our solidarity in God!

I delight in the time in which the Psalmist elected to pray to the God Whom he adored, and Whom he trusted in his personal comings-and-goings: 'the morning'. Starting so early, it was easier to get his priorities right. And this remains as true for you and me. One can, of course, reach out to God in prayer from anywhere, at any time – I am not one who insists that prayer be urged upon another first thing, as the *only* proper and worthwhile occasion. I have found prayer real at many different times. But this I must say: waking in the early morning, one's mind is fresher, and the new, unfolding pattern of the day lies ahead. I always pray on waking. I speak to God, in thanks, praise, adoration, and trust, before I speak to anyone around me. It is wonderful to do this – to waken to a steadying awareness of God, to feel that the day about to unfold is His day, the very air I breathe, His air. From everlasting to everlasting, He is Lord of all. He is Maker of each mountain height. He is the source of the life-giving sun that tints each new dawn. He it is Who not only creates and stabilizes each mighty mountain's strength, but decorates it with the sweetness and fragility of tiny wild flowers. He it is Who reaches out with steadfast love and mercy to those whom He has made throughout the whole earth, and with whom He seeks continuing fellowship. In the main, I find this easier to accept and understand in the morning than at any other time – there is then a sort of clean, clear call, and beginning again.

Morning, of course, does not always mean at the sun's

rising, when one is made aware of God; it can be in the morning of youth. Powers are then unspoiled; ears are alert; capacities are still developing. I smile a little to myself when I hear or read heavy-weighted references to the Pilgrim Fathers; for I have learned that of the hundred and one people on the little *Mayflower*, thirty-nine were actually under twenty-one years of age. Only two of the total company were over forty. They were young men – like their eternal Master. The 'morning' was in their spirit, as in His! Again and again He rose for prayer with His Father, whilst the heavy-hearted slumbered, and sometimes it meant going into the hills. He couldn't do without that morning worship known to the Psalmist, in a lesser sense and in an earlier time, and now known to you and me, in our own faltering experience. The calm magnificence which walked with Him constantly could never have been His by any other means; and that close, continuing delight in His Father's Will in the earth, must also have otherwise been unknown.

I never felt more certain of this than when, in Palestine, I climbed to a high spot and looked down over the waters of Galilee. Whittier's lovely hymn that we members of the Youth Movement of our church sang – and still sing – was then in my mind:

O Sabbath rest by Galilee;
   O calm of hills above,
Where Jesus knelt to share with thee
The silence of eternity,
   Interpreted by love.

With that deep hush subduing all
   Our words and works that drown
The tender whisper of thy call,
As noiseless let thy blessing fall
   As fell thy manna down.

Drop thy still dews of quietness,
  Till all our strivings cease;
Take from our souls the strain and stress
And let our ordered lives confess
  The beauty of thy peace.

If life is to be good, one thing we need to learn, with the Psalmist and our Lord, is the humble, prayerful use of mornings.

Seasonal Delights

Most of us, it seems, have a favourite season. Talk with a neighbour or friend as the year rolls round, and the interest will become seasonal. One will favour the freshness and eagerness of Spring; another, the riot and russet of Autumn; whilst yet another will declare that he feels most fit in Winter; and there are bound to be those who think there is no issue to settle – that without doubt Summer, with murmurous days and fields full to overflowing, is the best.

The Psalmist in Psalm 74:17 (RSV) is content to mention but two seasons, and he does this unforgettably. Addressing God, the Creator of all that he watches come and go, he says:

> Thou hast fixed all the bounds of the earth;
> *Thou hast made summer and winter.*

At first what he says disappoints me, it seems so limited. But soon I realize that, in saying this much, he has said a great deal. In his day, among the pagan peoples around him there was a belief that the opposite seasons of Summer and Winter were the creation of two rival deities. The sharp contrasts, it was claimed, simply supplied proof of their mutual enmity. Whilst the god of Summer desired to cheer earth-dwellers with sunshine, warmth, and well-clothed gardens, the god of Winter just as purposefully planned to curse the earth with stripped landscape, and short days of cold.

Shrugging off these pagan conceptions, the Psalmist delighted to state that the God Whom he worshipped, had made both Summer *and* Winter. He was a great God! And because He made them, *both were good*. This was an advance on the pagan conception.

It may be that he went no further – as I had hoped he might – because the seasons, as he experienced them, were not as marked as they are in my country. The East and the West are in this, as in a number of other things, markedly dissimilar. I can agree that there are things to delight me, being of God's creation, in both Summer and Winter; but then I go on to feel the same about the two seasons in between, Spring and Autumn.

There is something very special about that Spring which God has made for us – though it may be that as one grows older, and one's energies diminish, one might feel it a little difficult to keep up with the Spring. She is like a romping child. At that stage the kindlier, quieter Autumn is likely to be favoured.

Spring, of course, is the time of resurrection, the time of rising bulbs bursting in beauty – life from apparent death. I like the way John Drinkwater tells of this in his Spring poem *Miracle*. I think the Psalmist, had he had a like experience, would also have rejoiced in it:

> Come, sweetheart, listen, for I have a thing
> Most wonderful to tell you – news of Spring.
>
> Albeit, Winter still is in the air,
> And the earth troubled, and the branches bare,
>
> Yet down the fields today I saw her pass –
> The Spring – her feet went shining through the grass.
>
> She touched the ragged hedgerows – I have seen
> Her fingerprints, most delicately green;
>
> And she has whispered to the crocus leaves,
> And to the garrulous sparrows in the eaves.

Swiftly she passed and shyly, and her fair
Young face was hidden in her cloudy hair.

She would not stay, her season is not yet,
But she has reawakened, and has set

The sap of all the world astir, and rent
Once more the shadows of our discontent.

Triumphant news – a miracle I sing –
The everlasting miracle of Spring.

In this respect I am served more generously than the Psalmist, for I have the Spring, and the God Whom I worship has made it, as well as the Summer and Winter. It is a lovely gift, as one of our earliest statesmen, Bartholomaeus Anglicus, makes plain:

> Spring tyme is the tyme of gladness and of love;
> for in Spring tyme all thynge seemeth gladde,
> for the earth waxeth grene, trees burgynne and
> spred, meddowes bring forth flowers, heven shyneth.

I glory in what God makes in Spring, year by year, especially when I am in England, where the change is so dramatic. One moment Winter holds, and the next – Spring has broken gloriously. Primroses are in the woods and hedges, together with that miracle of blue which is bluebells adrift beneath the trees. It was at this turn of the year that Chaucer knew a stirring and wrote: 'Now longen folk to go on pilgrimage.' I once carried my haversack, walking day after day with a friend, down that very Way he went with his pilgrims to Canterbury-towne. And pausing to recall its joys, I know it now to be one of the most glorious experiences of my whole life. It was easy there to lift my heart with the kind of seasonal delight the Psalmist could never have fully known in either Summer or Winter. For Spring is such a generous, green gift.

And this is not to bypass the other in-between beneficence of Autumn. I have been in Palestine and the adjoining countries in the Autumn, but did not find it the fulsome season I knew it to be at home, even though the grain all golden was being gathered in. With us, maple trees in Autumn are hung with colour at the end of the garden – the loveliest gift of God at that season. Poplars are golden spires, pricking out the river's way along through the valley, and the store room for fruits and nuts is full. The days are shortening, shadows on the wall, as they gather in sparrows twittering, and migratory birds taking their leave. It is a gentle time, and one in which it is easy to bless God, the Creator the Psalmist adored in Summer and Winter. It seems strange that such beauty should accompany the withdrawal of life in branch and leaf – yet so God has made it. And my heart leaps at every experience of it! To be sure, the God we worship is a great God! Each season He casts His spell. He Who made Summer and Winter, rejoiced in by the Psalmist, gives Spring and Autumn, too. He sees the whole as clearly as any part.

In this glorious realization, St Thomas Aquinas's prayer rises naturally and gladly to my lips: 'Grant, most Merciful Father, that in Thy presence, my spirit may receive wisdom, and my powers of action the glory of triumph; *in Thy presence where there is . . . the charm of Springtime, the light of Summer, the fruitfulness of Autumn, and the repose of Winter. Amen.'*

Better Than Birds Sing

Do you ever waken especially to listen to the dawn chorus? I do. It's so fresh and so full of vigour. And I like to pick out the separate songs.

All through the morning, the thrush is my favourite. He is so joyous that he sings everything twice or thrice over. Somebody has written of this very charmingly:

> In through the open windows, loud and clear
>   and passing sweet,
> His message comes:
> 'Do you – Do you – Do you
> Give Him thanks, give Him thanks
> As we do, as we do, as we do?
> God! God! God! God! God!
> To Thee be thanks, to Thee be thanks
> For sunshine and Spring.
> I did it! I did it! I did it!
> Do you do it? Do you do it?
> He made you. He gave you
> Sunshine and Spring.
> Did you do it? Did you do it? Did you do it?
> Do it! Do it! Do it!
> Thank Him for everything!

That sounds like the thrush; and it sets one thinking of the Psalmists. Psalm 118 starts off: '*O give thanks unto the Lord*; for he is good; because his mercy endureth for ever.' Viscount Grey of Falloden, one of the keenest birdlovers of our time, once wrote a book, *The Charm of Birds*. He delighted to tell of his knowledge of them, and of the village church, where he gathered with others. Of one occasion, he said: 'We had the one hundred and eighteenth Psalm, and a fine chant for it; do you know the Psalm? *It is splendid . . . and says things two or three or four times over, because it is so glad.*' That's like the thrush. It lifts up one's heart. But it carries more meaning than the thrush can ever express, for men and women have a God-given capacity unknown to any bird.

And that experience of God calls for a degree of thanksgiving unknown in any other area of creation. In Psalm 136, in the Revised Standard Version, this is remarkably declared. Could it be the same Psalmist who began Psalm 118? We have no means of knowing. Here he begins, in a voice that continues later, without any break:

O give thanks to the Lord, for he
is good;
his steadfast love endures
for ever!

Let Israel say,
'*His steadfast love endures for*
ever.'

Let the house of Aaron say,
'*His steadfast love endures for*
ever.'

Let those who fear the Lord say,
'*His steadfast love endures for*
ever.'

(Psalm 118:1–4, RSV)

Not content with a limited repetition, as is the thrush, the Psalmist uses every single verse of Psalm 136 to express his thanksgiving, soon taken up by others. It soon became part of the worship of the people – and not only as a 'dawn chorus'. It opened with a summons chanted by a precentor of a choir, to 'give thanks to the Lord'. Then the original reason for this was gloriously extended. The motif throughout is His 'steadfast love'. This is shown in so many ways, beginning with the world He created. *His steadfast love is unending – and nothing known to men and women is so worthy of thanks.* Having repeated this reality more times than any singing bird, before he is fully done, the Psalmist exhausts his human power of expression, and so must make an end, twenty-six verses on.

> *O give thanks to the Lord,*
> *for he is good,*
> *for his steadfast love endures for ever.*
> O give thanks to the God of gods,
> for his steadfast love endures for ever.
> O give thanks to the Lord of lords,
> for his steadfast love endures for ever;
>
> to him who alone does great wonders,
> for his steadfast love endures for ever;
> to him who by understanding made the heavens,
> for his steadfast love endures for ever;
> to him who spread out the earth upon the waters,
> for his steadfast love endures for ever;

to him who made the great lights,
for his steadfast love endures for
ever;
the sun to rule over the day,
for his steadfast love endures for
ever;
the moon and stars to rule over
the night;
for his steadfast love endures for
ever;

to him who smote the first-born of
Egypt,
for his steadfast love endures for
ever;
and brought Israel out from among
them,
for his steadfast love endures for
ever;
with a strong hand and an outstretched arm,
for his steadfast love endures for
ever;
to him who divided the Red Sea in
sunder,
for his steadfast love endures for
ever;
and made Israel pass through the
midst of it,
for his steadfast love endures for
ever;
but overthrew Pharaoh and his host
in the Red Sea,
for his steadfast love endures for
ever;

to him who led his people through
the wilderness,
for his steadfast love endures for
ever;
to him who smote great kings,
for his steadfast love endures for
ever;
and slew famous kings,
for his steadfast love endures for
ever;
Sihon, king of the Amorites,
for his steadfast love endures for
ever;
and Og, king of Bashan,
for his steadfast love endures for
ever;
and gave their land as a heritage,
for his steadfast love endures for
ever;
a heritage to Israel his servant,
for his steadfast love endures for
ever.

It is he who remembered us in our
low estate,
for his steadfast love endures for
ever;
and rescued us from our foes,
for his steadfast love endures for
ever;
he who gives food to all flesh,
for his steadfast love endures for
ever.

Better Than Birds Sing

O give thanks to the God of heaven
for his steadfast love endures for
ever.

(Psalm 136, RSV)

In this the Psalmist, gathered together with his fellows, enumerates the mighty works of God, but more especially the lasting, loving, steadfast character that is His. Therefore, everything good He gives, and every need throughout human history, He meets. And together they sing – outdoing even the birds in repetition – as those who abide in 'the steadfast love' of the eternal, ever-gracious Creator God.

In our own day, Ralph Richmond, poet and author, in a busy nine-to-five life as a copy-writer, engaged on secular affairs, took time, a little while ago, to write briefly of what he calls 'my philosophy and my belief'. 'God,' he begins, 'made this world – in spite of what man now and then tries to do to un-make it – a dwelling place of beauty and wonder, and He filled it with more goodness than most of us suspect. And so I say to myself: "Should I not pretty often take time to absorb the beauty and the wonder . . . to contribute at least a little to the goodness? *And should I not then, in my heart, give thanks?*"

Ralph Richmond's question did not want an answer from him; and it shall not from me.

Over The Threshold

The one hundred and twenty-first Psalm is one of the best-loved – and also one of the most relevant today. It speaks of a vital faith, and ends with a glorious twofold summing up.

> I will lift up mine eyes unto the hills,
> From whence cometh my help.
> My help cometh from the Lord,
> Which made heaven and earth.
>
> He will not suffer thy foot to be moved:
> He that keepeth thee will not slumber.
> Behold, he that keepeth Israel
> Shall neither slumber nor sleep.
>
> The Lord is thy keeper;
> The Lord is thy shade upon thy right hand.
> The sun shall not smite thee by day,
> Nor the moon by night.
>
> The Lord shall preserve thee from all evil:
> He shall preserve thy soul.
> *The Lord shall preserve thy going out*
> *and thy coming in*
> *From this time forth, and even for evermore.*
>
> (AV)

There was once a time when life went on quietly – 'going out, and coming in'. But that is not so any more, even for small children. There is all too often, since mother has gone to work, no one to see them off in the morning, and no one to receive them back at their small day's end. And this is important, at every stage of life, through the teens, and on into maturity. Fortunately, religion, as Dr William Temple delighted to remind us, can cover all of life's happenings, on both sides of the threshold. He says of someone, 'he had no religious experiences, because all his experience was religious'. It was the confidence of the Psalmist: 'The Lord shall preserve thy going out, and thy coming in.' And a modern-day poet, Sara Teasdale, echoes it quite as confidently:

> It is all one, the coming or the going,
> If I have kept the last essential me.

But how can one keep 'the last essential me'? To that question, the Psalmist has the answer. It is: '*The Lord shall preserve thy going out, and thy coming in.*' For much of life is spent in crossing the threshold, going out to the many, and coming in to the few.

The threshold, in early times, was a very simple line in life, for many lived in caves. The lowly hearth was the centre of family life, the smoke escaping as it could. It was so in early Bible lands. The women made pots of clay, and used them in the preparation of meals. With bone needles they sewed garments and coverings from animal pelts, and in time wove wool from the sheep, and decorated themselves with crude bead ornaments. Men worked at their flint tools, both for hunting and for early agricultural efforts.

In a number of years, caves had largely given way to tent homes, or 'houses of hair', as they called them. They were a picturesque feature of Bible lands. Long after the tribes had ceased to be roaming herdsmen, and had become dwellers in small agricultural villages, the people were happy to return to their tents during the Summer harvest season.

Our homes, by comparison, are strangely sophisticated,

even the simplest of them. Yet still, the dividing line in human life is the threshold. On one side is 'the world within the world' – the sanctuary of love, the sheltered place where life's intimacies have a right, where children are born, and the secrets of life taught. On the other side of the threshold are neighbours, markets, roads stretching far. Crossing the threshold is no longer a simple undertaking, as it was at one time, when the shepherd went out to his little flock, and the vine-keeper to his vines. And when we have to cross the threshold, with the busy, modern day finished, radio, TV, mail, records, and newspapers have already arrived, and the telephone has been ringing. It is hard to find the peace and leisure that the Psalmist knew. So many voices bring us the world's concerns, and speed – within and without – complicates life. The Psalmist knew nothing speedier than a camel, or a horse, yet all our movement is swift, ever since progress brought us the combustion engine and the common use of electricity. To these have been added the plane, beyond the daily hazards and accidents of crowded ground traffic. At the workbench, and in the competitive dealing of big manufacturing and distributing firms, there is the harsh, competitive spirit; and in other areas of industry, the brutalizing of men's minds. For most of each day there is no recognition of eternal values, not even a denial of God. Instead there is a total spiritual vacuum as the normal mood of life. The battle is not only a battle for bread. For most of us the battle is to keep alive in our hearts the lasting truth that man does *not* live by bread alone.

Our going out, therefore, has elements unknown to the Psalmist in quieter, steadier, more leisured days. For no man or woman today is 'going out' easy – for some it is almost more than they can manage. Weariness of body and mind all too often – with standards lowered, compromises made, and many poor judgements – issue in grim accidents, personal hurt, even death.

The 'coming in' is also more complex. Wall-to-wall carpet, central heating, a refrigerator and deep freeze, added to an electric kettle and a list of other modern gadgets, in no way guarantees the ancient peace and family trust that earlier homes knew. Love, respect and fidelity are often lacking, and the inside of the marriage guidance office or the divorce court are known to all too many – with marriage vows forgotten, the children and teenagers of the family become scattered, having to face the loss of a sense of belonging. And nothing is so important to young and old. Wherever marriage is undertaken it is meant to the last to be more than 'a tired friendship'. Happy are those who know it to be so – who are aware of the blessing of God on both sides of the threshold. When that is so, whether in married or in single life, those of us so blessed, are rich indeed. Life is good. Home is the place where the most precious values reside, the best relationships, the most lasting satisfactions, the freshest fun. A good meal on the table is something – but the 'Threshold blessing' is more; home is home, and it reconciles us to lasting relationships, that the world outside can be faced with expectation and courage whatever tests it brings day by day. 'It is people, close-linked in unselfish relationships,' as my editor friend Dr Leslie Church loved to say, 'who make home; and it is the spiritual relationship of man to his Maker which gives him Home as the goal of all his pilgrimage.'

Home-makers today are, in many ways, different from the Psalmist, but at heart few things have changed. H. V. Morton, the famous traveller and writer, had no doubt about it. He said: 'The only things that change radically in life, are fashions and inventions. The human heart was patented long ago, and the Creator has not seen fit to bring out a later model.' The threshold of a camel-hair tent could know the blessing of the Psalmist, as could the later family home in a house of sunbaked mud, or firebaked bricks. These were there long before sealed roads and first class drainage came, and all the gadgets and conveniences that are ours today. But we are not as rich, unless at heart we know 'the Threshold blessing' of the Psalmist in simpler times: '*The Lord will keep your going out, and your coming in, from this time forth and for evermore.*' (Psalm 121:8, RSV)

Moments To Remember

The circumstances that brought me to two services in my church in one week – a baptism, and a wedding, in each of which *vows* were taken – has led me back to the Psalmist's words: '*I will pay my vows unto the Lord now in the presence of all his people*' (Psalm 116:14, AV). I cannot discover, at this late date, what kind of gathering it was at which he took his vows; but it must have been something as serious as the baptism and the wedding in which I so lately heard vows made. For to make a vow at all is a serious business. My dictionary defines it as 'a solemn utterance in the form of a promise to do some good thing hereafter'.

Vows are sprinkled freely all through the Old Testament. When Jacob went into Mesopotamia he vowed to God the tenth of his estate, and promised to offer it at Bethel (Genesis 28:20, AV). Laws were given to the people for the regulation and due execution of vows. A man might devote himself, or his children, to God. A vow had to be made deliberately and devoutly, for 'a sudden passion', said the law understandably, 'does not make a vow'.

I like the Psalmist's words, as I have given them. The kind of vow a man will make – and keep – shows very much the kind of character he is. There is an early word in Ecclesiastes, chapter 5:5, which underlines the seriousness of the undertaking: '*Better is it that thou shouldest not vow, than that thou shouldest vow and not pay.*' Surely that is fair, and clear enough. In another verse in the Psalms are these words: 'Make your vows to the Lord your God, *and perform them*' (Psalm 76:11, RSV). It is those last words on which the whole matter turns.

Vow-taking in our daily life today – apart from baptism

and marriage – is a slight matter, which is a pity. As Dr H. H. Farmer reminds us: 'The true vow is the attempt to capture the high and serious moment . . . to make it one of the permanencies of the soul's life, to condense out of the vapour of feeling a solid mass and momentum of directed will.'

Sometimes, of course, vows are made for us, as Wordsworth said very beautifully of his own baptism:

> I made no vows, but vows
> Were made for me; bond unknown to me
> Was given, that I should be,
>   else sinning greatly,
> A dedicated spirit.

Vows are the means by which one is carried above 'instinctive natural wants and desires'. Even in the days of the Psalmists it was so – and accepted thus into life. It is a shame that today we should anywhere lose this support by default.

One of the happiest memories of my time in the churches in Denmark, was in connection with the tiny votive-ships there. I lost much by my lack of language, but the reverence of my fellow worshippers, and the glory of the music which was part of worship, was real; and so was the setting in which I studied those small models, hanging often in the roof of a church. My eyes sought them out every time – the votive-ships skilfully and lovingly carved by men of the sea, and placed there on the completion of some undertaking on a voyage. The oldest votive-ship in the whole of Denmark is dated 1632, and is to be found in the church of St Morten, in Randers.

Before Reformation times the custom was widely followed in Britain, reaching away back to the Crusaders, who made their vows, and, on their safe return from the dangerous, fever-laden East, hung their votive-ships in their places of worship. But when religious zeal cast out stained-glass windows and medieval representations of the saints, votive-ships went too. In Germany, Spain, Norway and Sweden there are examples of them still, and also in the Groote Kerk in Haarlem, Holland. Whilst on a visit to the Dutch island of Marken, I talked with an old blue-jerseyed man of the sea. He was in his little house, preparing a meal – a typical Dutchman in his wooden clogs and baggy blue breeches. All his life, he assured me, he had worn the same kind of clothes, and all his life he had loved the sea. He had sailed out into the fishing grounds of the Zuyder Zee when it was blue and calm, and when angry storms had beaten up. But now, in advanced age, he was content to stay with the little pointed houses along the jetty-side, each painted bright green, blue or yellow.

We went together to the church. For some time, he had cared for it lovingly. He was not the Domine – he did not preach or teach – but he looked after the building, opening it in the morning, closing it safely at night, and keeping it clean and tidy for the services, when the congregation from all over Marken came to worship. His name, I learned, was Jan Peereboom.

I asked him about the votive-ships, hanging neatly in the roof of the church. Big ones and little ones, they were there above the heads of the worshippers, and each one, correct in every detail, had been made with the utmost care. The first was a lugger, about twenty-four inches long, gay with pennant and sail, and complete with fishing-net; the next was a sailing ship for catching eels; the third was a herring boat – a *buis* – one of the oldest boats of all. As I admired it, old Jan went into the vestry and brought out a picture of a fleet of *buis*, sailing out from Marken. 'Now there is only one left,' he said. I asked him: 'Was it in this kind of vessel that you fished?' 'Yes,' he replied, well content, 'for thirty-five fishing seasons I went out into the great seas in a boat like that.' And his old eyes shone, remembering all the hazards met.

When I asked why the church housed the votive-ships, he answered, as I expected he would: 'Because we have come back safely, our undertaking fulfilled, to the glory of God.'

In no church where I have regularly worshipped are there votive-ships, because none of us 'went down to the sea in ships', as the Psalmist says (Psalm 107:23, AV). But I could wish we had some outward and visible reminder of our own, of our inward and spiritual vow-taking. It might help. Each little ship in the churches I visited, in the strict dictionary sense of 'votive' had been '*offered, consecrated, and received* in fulfilment of a vow'. I was impressed to learn of a dozen new ones raised in the churches of Denmark during the very year that I visited the country. So the custom had not died out. There were about eight hundred altogether in the two thousand two hundred churches.

But we have the Psalms – and the words of the men who served God in earlier days are there to this day, to remind us of our vows and their resulting obligations. And they are striking words: '*Make your vows to the Lord your God, and perform them*' (Psalm 76:11, RSV). In the hymnal used in the church where I worship is a hymn with a verse that I have never yet heard sung – perhaps we ought to sing it, and often:

Here the vow be sealed
By thy Spirit, Lord;
Here the sick be healed,
And the lost restored;
Here the broken-hearted
Thy forgiveness prove;
Here the friends long parted
Be restored to love.

(*Methodist Hymn Book*, 981)

In True Fellowship

Early in the history of human life the Creator decreed that it was not well for man to live alone, and ever since, life has confirmed that wise judgement. Not only in marriage does this apply, but in the much wider realm of fellowship. The Psalmist's words stand out from the page, when one turns to Psalm 133: verse 1, in the Moffatt translation:

> How rare it is, how lovely,
> the fellowship of those who meet together.

We cannot know the experience of the Psalmist but he shows himself close to each one of us, in this. Loneliness is one of the most widespread sicknesses of our time. Doctors, ministers and social scientists all underline this word from the psychologists.

There is no way of discovering whether the Psalmist was a married man, or a member of a local society, or a regular worshipper along with others of like mind, when he wrote so tellingly about fellowship. But nothing has happened in our modern life, to outdate his finding. Fellowship is essential, if life is to be good.

Today, we use the term so glibly that we must needs pause to ask ourselves, in our chosen gathering: 'Is our fellowship a Fellowship?' We so easily use the term to describe our gathering together in one place. We speak of our 'Youth Fellowship', our 'Mothers' Fellowship', our 'Men's Fellowship', among others. But we cannot create fellowship by thus bestowing an inviting name on any gathering we achieve in any known place. For fellowship is so much more than proximity – than even the underlining of a common interest, even a religious interest.

Beginning with marriage – the joining together of two people, a man and a woman, in fellowship – Dr Max Warren quotes a definition in which fellowship is described as 'The joy of going through life hand in hand with the comrade of one's choice, sharing one another's burdens, stimulating one another's courage, doubling one another's sagacity, buckling on one another's armour, wearing one another's laurels, and easing one another's pain'.

'Fellowship is life, and lack of fellowship is death,' is the plain way William Morris put it, and he was not thinking necessarily of the marriage contract, however perfect on occasion. His statement reaches out also to those who elect to remain single, though that does not mean that they choose to remain solitary, much less lonely.

Church people talk a lot about fellowship, and sometimes, it seems, even mistakenly think they have a monopoly of it. Many of its gatherings are certainly designed to promote it: cups of tea, cosy gatherings, talking about the same things, listening to the same things, looking at life in much the same way.

But fellowship in its richest manifestation is a byproduct of an adventure in living – as is happiness. And it involves utter, honest, glad self-giving. It often starts in doing a piece of work together, very seldom by talking of fellowship, or by setting out deliberately to establish it. Such an undertaking tends to make for self-consciousness – and that is the finish of true fellowship. And, at the other extreme, fellowship means much more than being matey. In its true nature, it also reaches down to life's depths.

When I was growing up, I belonged to what we prided ourselves on calling 'A Fellowship Group'. We did all we knew to engender that precious experience; we even chose to sing a song which seemed, in its spelling, to belong to an early period:

Lo, here is Felawschippe,
One faythe to holde,
One troth to speake,
One loving cuppe to sippe,
And to dip in one dysshe,
Faithfullich as lambkins of onc folde.
Either for other to suffer all things,
One song to sing in swete accord
And maken melodye.
Lo, here is Felawschippe.

It was set to a fine tune; and it suggested a long-time search of the human heart. We imagined it to be an early expression of that lovely, essential experience underlined by the Psalmist. Had Dr Moffatt's Old Testament version, published in 1924, been known to us, we might have allied our Group song with the Psalmist's words: 'How rare it is, how lovely, the fellowship of those who meet together.'

For there were times when we really found what we sought. (Long after I had moved away from the city where our Group met, I chanced on the words we knew as an early song, printed in *John O'London's Weekly*, a literary magazine that fed my book-loving mind. And the following week, I read there a letter from one who could say that 'the lines first appeared at the beginning of *Long Will*, by Florence Converse', and thus, on the witness of this correspondent from Leicester, were 'written in modern times'. I was interested to have this information – but, of course, fellowship remains timeless; modern life, with its new forms of isolation, made it more than ever so. Loneliness is the modern hurt experienced by so many.)

The Church lays great emphasis on fellowship. It laid hold of a special word, *Koinonia*, for it, when the canon of New Testament Scripture was being put together. And that word still walks up and down in our hearts, and in Christian textbooks. Considering it, Christians of the Middle Ages liked to gather its truths and experiences up into one brief saying easy to pass from one to another: *'One Christian is no Christian.'*

When Paul wrote to his friends that they were 'called into the fellowship of His Son, Jesus Christ our Lord', he was going right to the root of the matter, reminding them of a self-giving first to their Lord, and then naturally to each other. Fellowship, he full knew, is vastly more than tacking a label on a group of people brought together. It is found in gatherings of various sizes, and often in unexpected places.

I had a telling experience as a Methodist, a European, when invited to visit a little Presbyterian Mission House in a vast isolated Maori area beyond Lake Wai-kare-moana, little known to most people. It was arranged that I should drive in over those rough, winding country roads during the early part of the day, speak to an invited company in the evening, and go on next day. The two women who directed work at the Mission House and day school, year after year, had done everything possible to make it a rewarding experience.

The first guest to arrive, after myself, was a tall, gentle, dignified Maori lady. She had come thirty-eight bush miles on a timber-wagon. As we were introduced, she came towards me with an outstretched hand. 'I got a lift,' said she, 'to meet you, and hear you speak.' Then standing at full height, she told why. 'I live in a quiet place,' said she, 'but I have your book *Through Open Windows*. When I heard you were coming, I knew we must meet.' Then after a pause, she added: *'For what is in you is in me – and what is in me, is in you!'*

With all our differences, that unexpected meeting spelled out for us both an experience of fellowship. The Psalmist is right: '*How rare it is, how lovely, the fellowship of those who meet together!*'

In Miracles Fourfold

Life for us today is much more sophisticated than for the man from whom Psalm 127 comes to us, but still we feel close to him, because his short Psalm centres around four essentials: *the building of a house*, which is his home; *the raising of a city*, in which life can be set for him through his working days; *sleep at the day's end*; and *the on-going life of his generation*. And he makes no effort to conceal what he believes to be the secret of success. From the very first verse, he speaks clearly:

> Unless the Lord builds the house,
>   those who build it labour in vain.
> Unless the Lord watches over the city,
>   the watchman stays awake in vain.
> It is in vain that you rise up early
>   to go late to rest,
> eating the bread of anxious toil;
>   for he gives to his beloved in sleep.
>
> Lo, sons are a heritage from the Lord,
>   the fruit of the womb a reward.
> Like arrows in the hand of a warrior
>   are the sons of one's youth.
> Happy is the man who has
>   his quiver full of them!
> He shall not be put to shame
>   when he speaks with his enemies in the gate.
>
> (Psalm 127:1–5, RSV)

First comes *the building*, between himself and the sky and the elements round about him. Year by year, in London, the importance of this is still underlined by holding the Ideal Home Exhibition. The Psalmist didn't think of doing such a thing; and his display would have been so simple, had he done so.

Even a hundred years ago, experts tell us, the average person's 'wants' were only eighty-two. Today, by the same reckoning, they are four hundred and eighty-four! For that very reason, we more than ever need the Psalmist's word. God is concerned with the building of each house, and the standards therein.

Then there's *the city*, and the bustling life that goes on there. For the Psalmist, it must have been a relatively leisured coming together. But it is far from that today; newspaper headings of industrial strife, drink, drugs, assault, and divorce are largely centred in our cities. All too few of us ask, as the Psalmist surely would have done:

> Why build these cities glorious
> If man unbuilded goes?
> We build in vain, unless
> The builder also grows.

Dr Edwin Markham, who penned this query for us, knew just as well as the Psalmist that we cannot have a great city without God, nor good and great men without our deep-down daily recognition of Him.

Next, in the Psalmist's thought, was *sleep* at the day's end. He couldn't have managed without it, of course, any more than can any one of us, spending eight of our twenty-four hours in sleep – in all, twenty-three years out of our three-score-years-and-ten. Today, especially in our busy towns and cities, noise is unceasing; when bus and car traffic pauses a while, along with the builder, and the man with the pneumatic drill, above the blatancy of telephone and doorbell, youths who urge motorcycles up paved inclines at top speed, and top racket. Many in our midst find it hard to lay hold of their full measure of sleep – the gracious gift of God, which is designed to dissipate the fatigue toxins caused by the day's mental and physical exertions. These toxins have their effect on the nervous system, with results all too widely experienced today. Doctors, chemists and psychiatrists report their findings; and sufferers who so far haven't sought qualified aid, swallow more and more sleeping pills to try to secure this precious gift.

'The psychologist,' Professor Fearon reminds us, 'adds his findings to that of the pharmacologist, the pathologist, and the physiologist.' Between them, they know not only the necessity of sleep, but its frequency and depth, and the changes in the brain due to diseases that interfere with sleep. They have even invented methods of measuring muscular, respiratory and electrical changes during sleep. And all this sounds very clever – till, at the end, they are obliged jointly to admit that *they don't really know what sleep is*. There was a great conference on the matter, a little while back, and Professor Fearon's learned paper on *Sleep: Its Mechanism and Meaning* became a BBC talk. Many more must have listened to it, than ever turn to God – as the Psalmist did – with thanks for this common miracle. We fall into the habit of taking for granted much more than he ever did. And we often leave God out of this wonderful gift altogether. One striking exception in our day says:

> Of all the thoughts of God that are
> Borne inward . . .
> Along the Psalmist's music deep,
> Now tell me if there any is,
> For gift of grace, surpassing this –
> 'He giveth His beloved Sleep'?

And these blessings do not end with a daily recounting, but merge into the centuries' blessings of *the on-going generations*.

Every remembrance of this continuing gift of God is worthwhile. We none of us stand isolated on our own feet – we belong to the generations. This design of God has never come home to me more fully, since I first happened upon it in this quartet of the Psalmist's thanks for common mercies, and the abiding need for God at the centre of all, when lying thinking, in my modest grand-parents' house at holiday time. (It was, incidentally, the only house in which I ever slept upstairs during my growing-up years.) Lately, I found myself recalling those pre-sleep ponders, and set down my thoughts in a poetic but more mature form which I entitled: *The Grand-parents' House*.

This old house – with all asleep but me –
never quite forgets that it was trees
once, under wide skies, breathing free,
each season, answering each breeze,
reduced now to a thin old-agèd creak.

Dear wooden house, I bring to you my praise
for your glad, sturdy roof by night,
and your windows and doors, through days
welcoming within sun's sweet light,
and breeze, through arpeggios of leaves.

How many have been born in this place,
I wonder, as I lie awake,
how many grown to mind and soul space
here, over the years, to face and shake
things, and to meet life's load with laughter?

(R.F.S.)

No one of the four common human concerns listed by the Psalmist can be the glorious reality it is meant to be, without the presence of God.

As A Guest Of God

Week by week, I stand amazed before the forty types of bread on display at our Food Market. The cheapest are golden-crusted, sweet and new, as welcomed to our table; others are in colourfully designed wrappings; some sliced, and in varying thicknesses; some brown, some wholemeal, some white. Chaucer would be astonished at their diversity – his poor widow ate only brown bread, and rough. For a time, only black bread was served lowly servants, below those who might eat brown. When the Middle Ages were fully come, a common loaf was 'maslin bread' – being 'Miscelin', meaning mixed. It was of wheat and rye for the most part, sometimes with a share of barley and oats.

I am not sure of the mixture of the Psalmist's bread at his early date, but there was one thing about it that I can only regret is not universally acknowledged today: that it was owned as of God's giving. This grows harder and harder as time goes by, and we are further separated from the soil. In Psalm 39:12, RSV the Psalmist's words addressed to God are unforgettable: '*I am thy passing guest*, a sojourner, like all my fathers.'

In New Testament times, coming nearer our own, men and women, young people, and children as soon as they could lisp a prayer, were taught to pray: 'Our Father . . . give us this day our daily bread.' Though mixed in a home-made clay bowl, and baked on a modest hearth, they knew bread came from God – even though, as a family, they had sown the seed, and tended and harvested it. Life was simpler, and it was easy to acknowledge oneself God's guest.

In time children were taught a little rhyme:

Back of the loaf is the snowy flour,
And back of the flour is the mill,
And back of the mill is the sun and shower,
And the wheat *and the Father's will.*

It came to us from God, by way of hard work on the farms on which we lived. We knew ourselves to be God's guests, because we could not do it alone, could not find strength to plough, till, sow, harvest. And we children helped with the stooking of the golden sheaves, careful to set them so that the wind would blow through. Later we 'crowed' on the rising stack – that is, we received one by one the sheaves carted to the growing stack, and tossed them across to the stack-builder down on his knees. As loaded carts continued to come from the fields, it was a hot job. But it was all part of God's plan to give. (In time the term 'bread' came to have a wider meaning, including meat and vegetables and fruits – all part of our food.)

And year by year, our delight was in gathering samples of all that we enjoyed, to hold our Harvest Thanksgiving in the Chapel on a set Sunday. The day before, we made our way there, burdened with full baskets, bags and boxes, with great golden sheaves and flowers to decorate pulpit and windows. Prize pumpkins, and curly marrows, polished apples, peaches with blushing sweetness, pears, grapes and brown pears and nuts were set out on shelves. A housewife – sometimes our own mother – counted herself honoured to be chosen to bake a great golden crusty loaf, cottage style, for the centre of the display; and some father brought a glass of clear, cool pumpwater from the secret places of the earth. We knew how much we depended on such things, not forgetting heaven's showers in the early stages of sowing and tending, even as later we depended on God for the sustained sunshine in the mellowing, ripening time of the harvest season.

Year by year, working under the hot sky, we retold with

laughter the story of the old Chapel-goer bothered about the weather. In a time of drought, he found himself praying; and then again, with some confusion, later, when prolonged dry weather eventually gave way to a sudden and continuous downpour. 'Dear Lord,' he began, 'last week we axed 'ee vur rain. And when we axed 'ee vur rain, dear Lord, we wanted dapper little showers like. But, O Lord, this is ridiklus.' But had the management of the weather been left in human hands, much worse confusion must have resulted.

More recently, we farming folk, who have grown up close to the soil, were shocked to read a report to a commission of the British Council of Churches. It said brashly: 'The farmer of today knows how to get good crops without praying over them.' Was this saying that the farmer had outgrown the attitude of the Psalmist? – that he no longer knows himself 'a guest of God'; that he is unlike his fathers, in this, wholly sufficient to himself? Was it being claimed that that long-used petition of the Lord's Prayer 'Give us this day our daily bread . . .' is now out of date in a day of high-powered tractors, and ploughs and cultivators off the factory floor; followed by chemical fertilizers, and with highly-powered binders, and threshers? The modern baker belongs to the right *union*, not necessarily to any church or chapel. But this is only part of the whole. However much we pride ourselves on these things, our modern mechanisms are not all. *Ours is God-given bread, we are 'guests of God'*, as all our fathers were, back to the beginning of time. We cannot afford to forget the early statement of Augustine, considering the Festival of Harvest, and the filling of our stomachs from that harvest: 'Without God, we cannot. Without us, God will not.' However modern our techniques, there is no contracting out of that relationship known to the Psalmist, and very humbly, gratefully acknowledged in the words of the Psalm I have found myself, in turn, delighted to say: 'I am thy passing guest, a sojourner like all my fathers.' There is nothing unique about my bread, nothing self-sufficient, though it comes to me through the Food Market for our coins, and by the work of a leading firm of bakers.

God has set within the framework of seasons, showers, sun, and gatherings-in, ample for His children's needs; but only on one daring assumption: that we live together in the earth *as one family*. It is just at this point that our world-religion and economy break down. Archbishop Temple's words remain true: 'It is a mistake to think that God is interested solely in religion. He is interested in bread. It matters to Him – because people matter to Him.'

Song In A Strange Land

It's easy to think of Bible happenings in terms of Bible pictures: a few people gathered, garbed in Eastern clothes, and gracefully arranged. But there was nothing either small or graceful about the fifty thousand people carried off into Exile in Babylonia, at the king's command. They were sternly required to live in colonies, and to do as they were bid.

And there was an ache in the heart of things. Some of that ache makes itself known to those of us who read the Psalms recounting that period. Their captors ridiculed them, and taunted them with a suggestion of song, when that seemed the very last thing that they wanted to do. Parts of their experiences were so grim. '*How,*' they cried, '*shall we sing the Lord's song in a strange land?*' (Psalm 137:4, AV). How indeed?

The outlines were harsh; the company they kept was not of their choosing; and when would this painful state of affairs finish? Would they then be able to return where they belonged? Meanwhile days and days dragged by; plans were undertaken, without their consent; energies and skills were spent on undertakings that meant little or nothing to them. They were subject to moods that others did most to make. How could any of them, at any time, sing, unless song rushed to their lips from glad hearts? – and they were anything but glad as they heard this command. How could they sing?

Perhaps their captors flung them the command to try to lift them out of their lethargy? Or maybe it was to deepen their homesickness, to remind them of the chosen life they had left? Either way, it was a cruel thing. They might have groaned, on hearing it – they might have cursed – but to sing? That was asking too much. Strange, godless lands were these into which they had been carried, and the very suggestion that the suffering people should sing the songs that over the years had meant much to them, to titillate the ears of those who multiplied their griefs, seemed a bitter joke.

And yet, they must have sung *some* of them, because they had no choice, since during that wicked, hard time, the songs lived on, and how could they have done that if all the people had kept silent? Maybe that was what some of their number felt: that hard circumstances were the very times when songs were most needed? One thing is certain – many people since, finding themselves in 'a strange land', have found strength and witness in song to be the greatest possible help to their own spirits, whatever might happen to those about them handling the lash. It came to an end, of course, in time. 'Alongside the harsh picture, and the voices choked with tears,' Dr Hastings reminds us, 'we must set this word: "When the Lord turned again the captivity of Zion, then was our mouth filled with laughter, and our tongues with singing."' Never had they sung quite like that before – there was a new quality in their tone. And we on the outside know how that came about – it was hammered out in a hard place. *The people had 'sung the Lord's songs in a strange land'*.

'A strange country' is not always a matter of geography, although for many today it is. They are refugees from war, political upset, economic failure, redivision of countries, even the blotting-out of the name of one's long-loved country; and carrying their pitiful little bundles, they traipse through vast places, ride in cattle-trucks like animals, or commit themselves to leaky boats to get out of Vietnam. And when they do stop, it's hardly likely to be where they want to be – it's 'a strange land'.

The question is, 'Can they sing a loved song in that situation?' Already over one-sixth of the coloured people in

Britain were born where they are – they are not immigrants, but coloured Britons. They are 'in a strange land', and they have to face experiences the rest of us have no knowledge of, not least of which is living within a coloured skin, which proclaims one a stranger. And this not in Babylon, where there are cruel masters and lashes. And many pious people don't altogether understand this. It has been written of someone, typical, one fears, of a good many:

> She spoke of heaven
> And an angelic host;
> She spoke of God
> And the Holy Ghost;
> She spoke of Christ's teachings
> Of man's brotherhood;
> Yet when she had to sit beside a Negro once –
> She stood.

But the 'strange land' where many of us find ourselves, is the land of human suffering. Its frontiers merge on those of home, then reach out to take in an unknown hospital ward; an X-ray theatre; a clinic; a convalescent home. And sometimes we are called on to pass a long time in any one of these. All sorts of thoughts go through our heads; time loses its meaning; life's centralities are bruised. Can we sing 'the Lord's song' in such a 'strange country'? We must, or else falter, and fail to win out. As hospitals, like social services, succeed, they should surely go out of business. But that isn't what happens – they seem to grow more and more in every town and city, spreading out ever wider. So very many in our day spend time in this 'strange land'.

And many suffer imprisonment, even torture in many South American and African countries. Amnesty International, whose newsletters reach me regularly, as an interested helper, has the names and details of many. The prisoner of the month, I see, is an attractive young person, one of twenty-two people who disappeared in Brazil during the early months of 1974. She is reported to have been tortured and held incommunicado ever since. Ann Silva, an assistant professor of chemistry at the University of Sao Paulo, was last seen by friends on 22 April 1974. Later the same day her husband, Dr Wilson Silva, disappeared on his way home from work.

Ann Silva's father, the well-known poet and writer, Mayer Kucinski, immediately made enquiries and was told by officials that neither his daughter nor his son-in-law had been detained by the government. He later learned through unofficial channels that the couple had been arrested by the Departmento de Ordem Politica e Social in Sao Paulo (May 1979).

What 'strange land' do those gifted young people share? Or do they still live?

Many survive prison; many write of their experiences, whilst still there; and what they have to say stirs our hearts. We know they are 'singing the Lord's song in a strange land'. Pastor Georgi Vins who wrote from the grim Lefortovo Prison in 1966 – and who was released only in 1979 – could say: 'Despite the very strict isolation . . . a link between the Christian prisoners is gradually established and functions successfully. I know about almost all the believers who are held here. *All are cheerful and steadfast in their trials for the faith.*'

Do you live in 'a strange land' – is there lack of fellowship? Or is there crippling illness? Or a secret hurt that you cannot share? But faithfulness to the highest one knows is possible in any 'land'. Sir Geoffrey Jackson, held captive for months by urban guerrillas, was ultimately freed in front of a Roman Catholic church in Montevideo. The astonished young priest to whom he made his confession, and received then the sacrament – followed by a cup of coffee – knew the reality of the situation. It was certain that God had been in 'that strange land', which for Sir Geoffrey had been but an underground cellar.

Again and again, the setting differs, but the capacity to 'sing there of spiritual realities', is unquestionably real.

Through Earth's Lovely Creatures

All the hours of day and night God's lovely creatures are busy. The Psalmist sings of them with delight:

> O Lord, how manifold are thy works!
> In wisdom hast thou made them all;
> *The earth is full of thy creatures.*
>
> (Psalm 104:24, RSV)

Bible lands have long valued these gifts of God, and many of them constituted their wealth in ancient times. As many as three hundred birds alone have been identified in the small land of Palestine. Sparrows were common enough, and everybody knew doves and pigeons, and they waited for the swallow and stork to come on migration. Partridges and quails were valued amongst the Hebrews. And there were also the animals close to their lives: the donkey, the ass, the awkward camel, oxen, cows, goats and flocks of sheep. In our century, John Galsworthy seems to be echoing the delight of the Psalmist, when he says: 'The world is dressed in living creatures.' And the twofold truth that we have to embrace is that it is God's world, and they are God's creatures.

Many of them have become domesticated, sharing life very closely. It must have been so where the Psalmist grew up; and certainly it was so in the farmhouse where I grew up. Friendly 'Four Paws', the family pussy, twisted herself around my legs first thing on rising; and as soon as I was free to move out of doors on to the nearest patch of grass, little sparrows waiting there came 'chissuping' cheerfully to receive their crumbs.

My first toy was a Noah's Ark – home-made at the cost of one-and-sixpence (seven and a half pence), my father told me later – made up of the price of three tiny cans of bright paint, red, green and blue. And ever since, I've loved creatures, providing they are allowed to be themselves, and are not talked to in sentimental words, and credited only with motives and responses proper to human beings. I can't imagine my Mr Noah and his wife and their three sensible sons Shem, Ham and Japheth, being so silly. Nor can I imagine the Psalmist talking sentimentally to God's creatures. It is true that in his day dogs lacked much of the attractiveness they have come to have for us. Then, they lived on the streets, and acted as scavengers, often making the night noisy with their fights. To call a man 'a dog' was a cruel insult; to leave the beggar at the rich man's gate to have his sores licked by the dogs, was to draw a word picture not as rare as you and I would suppose; to leave the dogs to pick up 'the crumbs which fell from the master's table', was not the pleasant domestic picture it is easy now to envisage. With time, things have changed – in most relationships of creatures and master and mistress, they have grown more kindly. Rowland Hill, by the last century, was able to speak for many besides himself, when he said: 'I would give nothing for that man's religion, whose dog and cat are not the better for it.' This judges severely those who, in times not long past, set cocks to fight each other as a form of recreation; or caught seagulls on fish-hooks; or kept little pit ponies underground till they dropped in the darkness from sheer fatigue.

But many lovers of creatures have come to the fore since then, and compassionate laws have been made. We still have much to learn: for at every holiday, cats and dogs are left unprovided for, and must themselves forage for what they need. This is a sin against God, and against His creatures. Others are lovingly, responsively cared for. Whilst staying with us, an English friend received news that Grocy had died, and Grocy was a very special cat, a creature of God – at least to her little four-year-old mistress. The sad news was softened by the belief that somewhere, somehow, all is well with Grocy, that 'He's in the Never, Never Land, and he eats *lots* of fish and jumps for joy!'

I don't know about the hereafter, as far as God's creatures are concerned, but I trust Him to do the suitable thing for them. I haven't the confidence of John Hailsham, and scores of others, in a Dogs' Heaven. I have visited the Dogs' Cemeteries in London and in Edinburgh. I found another in the garden behind Carlyle's house in Chelsea – the well-marked resting place of a faithful dog. But little graves alone do not argue immortality, only loving concern. Under the trees in our farm garden, was added from time to time, another well-tended creature's grave. Sir John Lucas wrote, as an adult lover of his dog: 'In some canine Paradise your wraith, I know, rebukes the moon.' But we have no proof – it may be wishful thinking, which seems a fair reward for creaturely fidelity and companionship. Creatures, though we are very fond of them, lack the powers of personality that we can be sure persist. Such belief, as my friend Teresa Hooley has shared in her poem *Heterodoxy*, expresses at least a loving care for God's creatures that one can heartily approve, and a certain wistfulness. Says she:

In my Father's House are many mansions.
  Will there be room for all
His lesser children of field and forest,
  Kennel and byre and stall?

From a dog's soft eyes looks a soul undying –
  Love, service, loyal endeavour;
On the dusty back of a patient ass
  Christ's cross is stamped for ever.

Surely St Peter, cock on shoulder –
  The bird that saved his soul –
Will open the gate to fur and feather,
  Elephant, eagle, mole.

St Jerome will walk with a pride of lions,
  St Agnes will lead her lamb,
St Anthony's pig will trot beside him,
  Behind young Isaac's ram.

They of the Ark will follow Noah,
  And all come trooping in –
Each part of the consciousness of God,
  And each one free from sin.

They shall crouch at the foot of the Great White Throne,
  They shall drink of the crystal spring,
And every bird of the air shall nest
  In the shade of St Francis' wing.

I can only be sure of *this* life, and the responsibilities we each hold here. Our religion, as Rowland Hill underlines, ought to be expressed in our compassionate concern for God's creatures. And that's a charge against many who show contempt for them, in any way. Wordsworth is right:

> He who feels contempt
> For any living thing, hath faculties
> That he hath never used . . .

Today, even in my own country, many species are dying out because of growing contempt, and greedy carelessness – and, dare one say, lack of religion? It is well to impress on children in their earliest relationships with 'earth's lovely creatures' this call for care. Mrs Forrester and her little boy stood on deck, as they returned to New Zealand after two years in Sydney, Australia. The time for them to join Mr Forrester, who had gone ahead, had come. And down the wharf moved two camels led one behind the other. The first was put into a horse-box, but whilst being hoisted, the poor creature let out a pitiful protest. And its mate, still on the wharf, was no more willing to go aboard. For the next two hours, five men struggled with it. At last, one of the five went off and got a quantity of carrots. Then a lasso was procured, and winding it tightly about the unhappy animal's middle, it was eventually hoisted aboard. The camels had been brought from the desert areas of Western Australia, and were headed for the Wellington Zoo. Every morning, Mrs Forrester told me in a letter later, she and her little boy went down to see the camels. 'We felt,' she said, 'that we owed them a little respect.' I liked that – and I'm sure the Psalmist would have delighted in it. 'On reaching Wellington eventually, where we were to live,' she was happy to add, 'we went often to visit the exiled camels.'

In that mood, I come back to the words of the Psalmist, in a total Psalm that continues to bring me delight 'through earth's lovely creatures':

> O Lord, how manifold are thy works!
> In wisdom hast thou made them all;
> *The earth is full of thy creatures.*

The Strength Of My Life

As odds-and-ends of material are stitched together for the floor of a child's playhouse, so one stitch or more of a fragmentary Psalm is added to another. It is required only that the enlarged whole be in much the same mood. Psalm 27 is an instance, and here scholars can see the join: the first six verses make up one piece, and verses 7 to 14 another. 'The contrast between them,' says *The Interpreters' Bible*, 'is so well marked that it seems best to assume that we have here two originally independent psalms which, through circumstances at which we can only guess, have in their transmission, become joined together.' Let us here notice, in detail, the first part only:

The Lord is my light and my salvation;
  whom shall I fear?
The Lord is the strength of my life; of whom shall I be
    afraid?
When the wicked, even mine enemies and my foes,
  came upon me to eat up my flesh,
  they stumbled and fell.
Though an host should encamp against me,
My heart shall not fear:
Though war should rise against me,
In this will I be confident.
One thing have I desired of the Lord, that will
    I seek after;
That I may dwell in the house of the Lord all the days of
    my life,
To behold the beauty of the Lord, and to enquire in his
    temple.

For in the time of trouble he shall hide me in his pavilion:
In the secret of his tabernacle shall he hide me;
He shall set me up upon a rock.
And now shall mine head be lifted up above mine enemies
round about me:
Therefore will I offer in his tabernacle sacrifices of joy;
I will sing, yea, I will sing praises unto the Lord.
(Psalm 27: 1–6, AV)

It is a confident little song, all its brave spirit centred on the Psalmist's assurance expressed in one line: *The Lord is the strength of my life.* This was something much more than a man's muscle; it was something that goes on all through life, matching situations. He mentions many things that, but for this wonderful provision, would have struck certain defeat into his days. Much of his time might have been spent in fleeing from those who terrified him.

It is notable that he does not claim that no danger or difficulty has happened to him – life is still full of danger, but he is able to meet it. God is never satisfied to keep His favourites in safety – far from it. For example, some of the most hazardous experiences that have visited men, down through the centuries, have been the lot of Joseph cast into a pit by his jealous brothers; Nehemiah, ridiculed and obstructed in every possible way as he set his heart and energies to rebuild his beloved city; the stripling David, with his few smooth stones out of the brook, confronted by the size and bluster of Goliath; Job, in the midst of sickness and repeated disasters and losses; Daniel cast into a den of hungry lions. But each – though his circumstances varied greatly – possessed that strength of the Lord known by the Psalmist in his day. Time and location make no difference: God's strength, freely given, is undiminished.

Certain of the Psalms seem to suggest that God guarantees absolute safety to His chosen ones, and Psalm 91:7 is a case in point. 'A thousand,' it says, 'shall fall at thy side, and ten thousand at thy right hand; but it shall not come nigh thee.' This strikes us oddly, in terms of 'the pestilence that walketh in darkness; and the destruction that wasteth at noonday'. We can only credit those words for what it seems they say, when we remember that they are part of *a continuing revelation*. By the time the New Testament era dawned the attitude to desired safety was very different. Religion could not, in the acceptance of any such promise, be taken to add up to an insurance policy.

And in the time since, the established attitude among Christians is increasingly true. In childhood, I used to sing, as I lit my little bedtime candle and carried it into the velvety darkness of the unknown:

God keep us safe this night,
 Secure from all our fears,
May angels guard us as we sleep,
 Till morning light appears.

But I had to grow up and cease to be concerned with physical safety above everything. And, after the problem had partly resolved itself, through my teenage New Testament reading, the time came when I saw that Rupert Brooke, my poet hero, had written his own advanced idea on this:

War knows no power. Safe shall be my going,
Secretly armed against all death's endeavour;
Safe though all safety's lost; safe where men fall;
And if these poor limbs die, safest of all.

When I first knew World War II, with many close friends involved, it was to know that no parent on parting, no air force, naval or army chaplain, could read that Psalm 91 passage about safety, to servicemen and women.

We had to begin to reckon from the New Testament, and the words of Jesus, our Lord. When He took leave of His close friends, it was not to ask God to keep them physically safe, though He dearly, strongly loved those men! He had to pray, 'Not that Thou wilt take them out of this world [to a place of safety, where all will be well] but that Thou wilt *keep them within* this world' [brave, and dependable]. Clearly, He asked no guarantee of safety for them; indeed, two of them came to an untimely death – Peter even being crucified, although, counting himself utterly unworthy to be in any way like his Master, he met death head downward. James's death is shrouded in unknown circumstances save only that we know that he died cruelly and prematurely. The historian Eusebius was moved to quote from Alexandria a treasured tradition that the accuser of James, when his turn came, was so struck by his courage and general bearing during his accusation, that he declared himself a Christian, too. Presently, he too was carried off to execution along with James, asking the forgiveness of the apostle, which he received there and then, with a kiss and the words: 'Peace be unto you!'

I still remember the time during World War II when news reached us that the *Dorchester* had been torpedoed and lost. We learned that four gallant chaplains had gone down with that ship, voluntarily taking the places of men without life-belts. One of them was Clark Poling, the son of Dr Daniel Poling, the Christian editor. Before taking leave of his family, he had written to them: 'I know I shall have your prayers, but please don't pray that God will keep me safe. War is a dangerous business. *Pray that God will make me adequate.*'

That prayer was magnificently answered – he, with his colleagues, was adequate. It was *'the strength of the Lord'* which dwelt within them during that test. This glorious gift is always far greater than safety. 'Fear not them that kill the body,' are the words of Jesus, our Lord, 'and after that have no more that they can do!'

Setting A Price

Buying and selling has been part of life for a long time. Do you remember how you used to 'play shops' as a child? I do. It was my earliest known advantage in being a twin – we were always able to supply a 'shopkeeper', and a 'customer'. From time to time, we switched roles.

But we never dreamed that men and women would value other men and women so little as to sell *them*. Then we heard of Joseph, in our early Bible stories, sold by his brothers to a passing caravan – and similar sales have been made up through the centuries, with slavery supported. These debased values served as background to a striking statement by the Psalmist, who said of God's mercy to those unhappily involved:

> He pities the forlorn and weak,
> he saves the life of the weak,
> rescuing them from outrage and oppression –
> *they are not cheap to him.*
>
> (Psalm 72:13–14, Moffatt)

Whether we think of man in his early environment – part of the first expression of conscious life, gradually growing up, responding to God and life about him – or as man today, engaging in business transactions, walking on the almost total earth, and now on the Moon's surface, we are troubled. From childhood up, the accepted values of life in many parts of the world are very low. We stage an 'International Year of the Child', and then have to admit 'the sins of parenting' – to use an awful piece of jargon – that is, of being a parent. And where should we reckon on the right to count true values? UNICEF claims that in this very year, up to ten million children suffer severe starvation; as many as eighty million are exposed to starvation in a less severe form; and a hundred and twenty million around the world go to bed hungry, uncared for. This is selling children into physical, intellectual, emotional and spiritual poverty. Life can never be for them the rich thing it was meant to be. Where young life is deprived and growing life manipulated, it must always result in a bitter deal. Henry Labouisse, Executive Director of UNICEF, says to us words we ought not to forget: 'The International Year of the Child will have succeeded if it sets in motion plans and programmes that will improve the fate of generations of the children to come . . . We know that the world has the means. The question is: "Do we have the will?"' And deep down we have to find an adequate answer. God looks at these whom He has created, and in the words of the Psalmist: *They are not cheap to Him.* We overhear leaders of today's nations saying: 'Children are our most cherished possession.' But are they? How far have we come from the earth's early days, when all human life, from childhood up, was cheap?

In early Roman times, we find Seneca speaking and writing boldly, in a way that now horrifies some of us – and ought to horrify all of us, if we reckoned values, as the Psalmist did, in the sight of God. But Seneca didn't reckon values that way. Said he: 'We slaughter a fierce ox, we strangle a mad dog, we plunge the knife into sickly cattle,' and in the same breath he adds, 'children who are born weakly and deformed, we drown.' And Cato, another Roman, went on just as confidently, but sinfully, giving advice to one ready to sell: 'Look over the livestock and hold a sale. Sell your oil if the price is satisfactory, and sell the surplus of your wine and grain. Sell worn-out oxen, old tools.' 'Fair,' you say. But he goes on to add tragically: 'Sell an old slave, a sickly slave, and whatsoever is superfluous.'

And this dreadful page of world history called 'Slavery' involved some of the finest families in our nations, when men and women were sold for meagre, hard cash. Or they were sold into cheap labour – which was just as damning. In the north of England there still exists a plaque in a coalmining village, recording a disaster of 1832 and showing twenty-three names of those who died miserably underground. That was bad enough – but the greater tragedy is that all twenty-three of those who lost their lives – precious in the sight of God – *were under the age of nine years*! Robert Clark, responsible for that colliery, was not alone in selling young lives for gain, and it took a long time to waken directors of companies to an awareness of values as they were in the sight of God.

Little by little, the truth that the Psalmist underlined came to be accepted. In school we learned the names of some of those who fought slavery, and of those who opposed cruel working conditions in factories, workrooms, and shops, and anywhere that buying and selling went on. But there were others. I did not know of the contribution of one of them till I walked in the great north of England city of Liverpool, and came on a monument in some public gardens. Since then, I have read all I can about him. His name was William Rathbone, and he was a wealthy Member of Parliament, but with a true standard of human values. His idea of the worth of persons – as valued by God – showed early to those about him when his wife was taken very ill. To help care for her, he called in a nurse by the name of Mary Robinson, and there weren't many such nurses in those times. Nurse Mary Robinson did everything she could in William Rathbone's home; nothing, night or day, was too much bother. But, sad to say, at the end of months, her patient died. William Rathbone was heartbroken, but his pity was not for himself alone. He began to think of all the countless homes in that one great city, not to mention any others, where there were desperately sick people, with no money to summon help of any kind. And he wondered what he could do. At last, he approached Mary Robinson with a request: 'Would you go round from door to door in this city, and wherever there are sick folk, go in and nurse them? I'll pay you. Just for three months' trial?'

Nurse Mary agreed; and she found so many in need, that soon she was worn out. She returned to William Rathbone, told him everything, and asked if he could let her off and forget their undertaking together. But he could not. And after three months, Nurse Mary Robinson was herself won over – for by this time she had seen so many sick and worried people, and their children, coaxed back to full health and enjoyment of life. Digging even more deeply into his bank account, William Rathbone decided to engage several more nurses for such work in the needy city. However, nurses were so scarce that he decided to open a special training centre, and so the Liverpool Training School and Home for Nurses came into existence. It was a great success, and within six years there were trained district nurses in eighteen areas of Liverpool. Other cities soon began to copy, and in many parts of England, there are now district nurses – or Queen's Nurses, as they are called. This all goes back to essential human values, as underlined by the Psalmist. Ordinary nurses, ministering to ordinary men and women and little sick children; but the great truth remains true: 'They are God's people' – and *They are not cheap to Him.*

God has given us each a lasting standard of values for our fellows, and for ourselves. In this world in which we find ourselves, a person of any age, in any place, is an important creation of God. The fundamental fact is that each, in turn, is made by God, in His own image. True values are not those of the market place, but of a living soul's worth.

At A Loss For Words

There are times, oddly enough, when many of us are surprisingly dumb. That is so even at home, within the love relationship, and is no less so in our religious life. This latter state proved a sad lack in the Psalmist's day. He was moved to begin what is now Psalm 107 (RSV), with unforgettable words:

> O give thanks to the Lord, for he is good;
> for his steadfast love endures for ever!
> Let the redeemed of the Lord *say so*,
> whom he has redeemed from trouble
> and gathered in from the lands,
> from the east and from the west,
> from the north and from the south.

Why are we so often wordless? Is it because our religious experience is unreal? Dr J. B. Phillips, observing and writing today, wonders about this, much as the Psalmist did long ago. 'Many men and women today,' he says, 'are living, often with inner dissatisfaction, without any faith in God at all. This is not because they are particularly wicked or selfish or, as the old-fashioned would say, "godless", but because they have not found with their adult minds a God big enough to "account for" life, big enough to "fit in with" the new scientific age, big enough to command their highest admiration and respect, and consequently their willing co-operation.' Dr Phillips did what he hoped would help to mend this matter, by writing a book for such people, with the title: *Your God is Too Small* (Epworth Press). However one thought of God in childhood and youth, before struggling with the terms *Omnipotence* – ascribing to Him almighty power, adequate for the creation and maintenance of this vast universe in which we find ourselves; *Omnipresence* – underlining that to His unfettered being no place is near or far away, but all equally, readily at hand; and *Omniscience* – admitting the amazing reality that all things past, present and in the future are equally part of God's knowledge – He is a great God.

To test their concept of God, some young folk were lately asked a surprisingly modern question, which struck them as being an unreligious one: Do you think God understands radar? In nearly every instance their answer was 'No'. Subsequent discussion revealed the fact that these lively young moderns had not grown up in their relationship to God. If they had left behind the 'Grand Old Man' idea, they were not ready to say so: God still had a beard as early Old Testament pictures showed Him. Is that perhaps still our trouble, yours and mine? For surely there is a vastly more relevant answer awaiting: 'Let the redeemed of the Lord say so.' Have we grown too casual to rise to that direct challenge?

We have to find room for what people like ourselves can know of God – and 'say so'. This is His world, and He is a great God! Every hour of life here confirms it in this world created in time; created by a supremely intelligent mind; and plainly created for an amazing cause. Knowing even this much, how can we keep silent? No wonder the Psalmist is led to stir up the unreasonably dumb amongst us. The Psalmist's word is *Say so*! My choice crippled friend, poet Jane Merchant, found – or so it seemed to me when she shared it with me – the kind of statement that would have satisfied the Psalmist, if words about God are ever adequate. The more life teaches us of Him, the more we have to go on 'saying so'. So far, I haven't had any reason to dispose of Jane's affirmation:

God of distances,
God of here,
God of eternity,
God of now:
To be aware of Thy presence
Is Life.
To be aware, with yearning, of Thy absence
Is almost Life.
To be unaware of Thy presence, or of Thy absence,
Is Death.

We would be very different people, if we could find words to share gladly and growingly what we discover about God as we pass through this glorious business of living. Experiences come to all of us – experiences that would heighten and deepen both those of us who might share them, and those with whom they are shared. Dr H. H. Farmer, distinguished Christian scholar and speaker of our day, feels this as sincerely and practically as the Psalmist, or as any one of us who has given thought to it. 'If,' he says, 'we could remind ourselves every morning, if we could seriously accept what in our hearts we know, that every noble impulse, every aspiration for righteousness, every call to service, is indeed the personal touch of the living God . . . pressing in upon us and seeking to lead us higher, it would make us very different people.'

Why, then, do these rich experiences that come to us not issue in words – in witness to one person here and to another there, people needing above everything, in this world of on-going life, just exactly what we might share? What holds us back – is it shyness, or lack of reality? *Why do we not 'say so'?*

The Psalmist would be at a loss to account for our dumbness, as would many others, prophets, preachers, saints and ordinary people, from those early days when it cost often life and limb to 'say so'. But those who witnessed to God were men and women of magnificent faith. No cost was too much. In the eleventh chapter of the book of Hebrews stand many names, brought forward from the Old Testament times shared by the Psalmist, to what we now call 'The Westminster Abbey Chapter' of our New Testament. One by one, they are an inspiration. 'Wherefore,' is the summing up, 'seeing we also are compassed about with *so great a cloud of witnesses*, let us lay aside every weight' (that is, everything that crops up to hinder our witness, our power to know God's greatness, and to 'say so') for this is 'the sin which doth so easily beset us'. In actuality, we are called to join that illustrious company.

And it is not solely a challenge to those of us specially endowed with a shining gift of words – teachers, preachers, writers – far from it! For the challenge is not only to 'say so' in words (as some find it difficult enough to do, anyway), but in deeds!

When the modern German witness, Pastor Martin Niemoeller, was in our country, he told some of us of an unforgettable experience. He was in the concentration camp of Sachsenhausen, when a visitor called to see him. It was on the eve of Good Friday, and he had words to share. To reach him, Niemoeller had to be led from his cell to the administration building, and as he made his way thither he had to pass a hut wherein was an old friend, a fellow pastor. He was denied words, but as he approached Niemoeller saw that his friend had moved from words to deeds, and strikingly so: he had scratched in the gravel one word *VIVIT – He lives!* And it was a wonderful witness to God's loving revelation in Christ.

You and I have to find our own way of 'saying so' in deeds. Dr Niemoeller's friend knew well one of the most penetrating verses in the New Testament: 'Let us put our love not into words or into talk but into deeds, and make it real' (1 John 3:18, Moffatt).

We walk to and from church; but more often – several times more every week of our lives – we walk to and from our place of work, and there we mingle with people who, having little or no chance of listening to our words, must take account of our deeds. They know if we are Christian, if we are members of the Church, if what we claim rings true. Deeds tell them that – and deeds are very telling. I would not totally agree with old John Lydgate, back in the fifteenth century, but I think – as a woman of words – that I know what he was trying to say. Said Lydgate: '*Woord is but wynd: leave woord and take the deede.*' However beautiful words are, they are not all. To 'say so', in the most glorious sense, we need deeds too! And here and now, that challenge comes!

In The Good Earth

Have you ever possessed a piece of land? Or walked in a tree-filled garden about your house? Or lifted up your gaze on rolling acres that you farm or use for a livelihood? To such of us who have, the words of the Psalmist come very aptly, as for example in Psalm 24:1–6, where he sings: 'The earth is the Lord's' – and we need to say in this ground-greedy day, '*not the landlord's*!'

The earth is the Lord's and the
  fulness thereof,
 the world and those who dwell
  therein;
for he has founded it upon the seas,
 and established it upon the rivers.

Who shall ascend the hill of the
  Lord?
 And who shall stand in his holy
  place?
He who has clean hands and a pure
  heart,
 who does not lift up his soul to
  what is false,
 and does not swear deceitfully.

He will receive blessing from the
  Lord,
 and vindication from the God of
  his salvation.

Such is the generation of those who
seek him,
who seek the face of the God of Jacob.
(RSV)

More and more this challenge of stewardship needs to be underlined. The earth as God dreamed it, and gave it, was unspoiled. Day after day, in the record of its creation, we read, 'God said, "It is good!"' (first chapter of Genesis). But it did not long stay like that. It may have begun to give trouble in the Psalmist's day, or one wonders why he spoke so boldly. Did he see God's earth mistreated? Modern research assures us that the waste area of the Sahara was not always as now. Successive generations of nomadic farmers and dealers ignorantly cleared the protective forests, leaving a trail of destruction in their wake. Parts of Africa that once offered homes to many, are now wastelands, graveyards of effort, directly as the result of forest destruction. And many strips of the prairies are but a dustbowl, after ruthless burning and uprooting. Year by year, the Yellow River swirls away to the sea tons of soil, on which families might still live. And our Australian and New Zealand pattern of erosion is only a little less tragic. Ignorance and selfishness have to be reckoned at a high rate, in the economy of the Creator. We cut down trees, alter the severity of the rainfall and send God's good earth coursing down the steep hillsides, into His rivers and out to His seas. And a kind of logging goes on, in many parts, with no greater a sense of stewardship. There is a verse in the New Testament, for those who pass the Psalmist's words without attention: 'Hurt not the earth . . . nor the trees!' (Revelation 7:3, AV). It's not just a matter of money – a matter of family, and business, greed. It should be carried forward into our Christian teaching, as the most obvious area of stewardship. It is a quality of life that is in question.

'Why,' asks Donald K. Faris of the UN Technical

Assistance Administration, 'is there not enough food to go round? Why is it that certain areas of the world are producing fifteen to twenty times as much food *per capita* as others? The answer to these queries,' he says, 'is bound up with three vitally important factors which must be taken into consideration if we are to make a correct evaluation.

'The first is availability of land. There are those who estimate that an average 2·5 acres of arable land are necessary to produce an adequate diet for each individual. Others debate this figure, stating there are too many variables affecting the yield – climate, fertility, and such like – to make any right calculations possible. We do know, however, that in areas where there are large surpluses of land, as in North America, with its 3·5 arable acres for each person, there is little hunger; while in a country like Egypt, people must eke out their total subsistence on one-fifth of an acre – or perish.'

Then this expert, Donald K. Faris, talks about the point we have already made: the relative conservation, and waste of acreage in God's good earth. Natural forest, cultivable soil no longer held in stewardship. Winds should not be allowed to blow over soil and rock, till they are bereft of the possibility of growth. *For this is God's earth.* In many country places in most productive countries, there are humble men and women who understand this. They know they are answerable to God for what they plough, and sow, and harvest. Frank Kendon spoke well of one such, who ploughs now the land his father ploughed in his lifetime:

> He watched this land;
> He drove this plough:
> He cast the corn
> I harvest now.

This is the land
My father tilled,
And my son shall
When I am stilled.

The man who follows the lead of the Psalmist knows that he is not only responsible to God, Whose earth he tends – but that he is responsible too for what he has, and what he is. It involves his whole personality, wherever he is in God's earth. Much has been given to him – and much can reasonably be expected. This is the on-going pattern of stewardship.

And as a third essential, Donald K. Faris talks about 'irrigation, cultivation, and improved seed and stock, disease and insect control'.

Far from being out of date, the words of the Psalmist come to us with an urgency that we cannot ignore in this hungry age. And every one of us in any way serving the earth, or drawing daily sustenance from it, has a duty to God and to the human race. Stewardship is not just wheedling more money from what grows; it means the honest examination, and honouring, of our traditional attributes. Life in this great earth of God's is never static – something is going forward, or backward, all the time. Such stewardship can't begin too soon, or stretch too far. We have all to learn to pray in a real way: '*Our* Father, give us this day our daily bread . . . *Our* Father . . . *our* bread . . .' And we need to join with others who dedicate themselves in this glorious continuing purpose in God's earth, as *brothers*.

Dr W. E. Orchard would lead us to pray:

O God, Whose hand is hidden in the framework of the world, shines in the mind of man, and is made flesh in Jesus Christ; we have heard Thee calling us by name, and like sheep to a shepherd, children to a father, we come to Thee.

In every age men have heard Thy voice, and we can hear it still. We catch its accents in the whispering wind and the sighing gale, its music in the ray of the stars and in the light of day. Beneath the hum of the world's vast work, and beyond the clamour of men, it soundeth to us. And when we shut our eyes or stop our ears, it calleth louder still within.

We have journeyed far, but Thy voice has followed; we have been careless, rebellious, and sometimes tried to drown Thy call; but as we dared to hearken, it came back again, and is with us to this hour.

We know we can never roam where that voice will not follow, nor shall we ever try again; for we know it leads to joy and rest, to happy service and to perfect freedom. We know it is the voice of love beyond imagination or desire, the call of a heart that feels and cares.

So long, so late, and many of us so sad, yet at last we come . . . Amen.

God's Grace

As a healthy, hungry child, I early learned the meaning of 'saying Grace'. But I was for some years mystified to hear the preacher on Sunday talk about 'The Grace of God'. Plainly, it had nothing to do with beginning a meal. In time, my music teacher introduced me to 'Grace notes'. It seemed that they were extra notes added to a simple melody to make it nicer. That was how she explained it to me. When I looked it up in my dictionary, it said very much the same: 'Grace notes are the embellishment of extra notes, not essential to harmony or melody.' So I have been slowly learning, all my life, that Grace is something good, something rich added to a situation; and in the case of God, out of sheer *graciousness*, it is loving generosity. I'm still learning, in heart and mind, what that means.

'Read the one hundred and third Psalm' is how Dr Leonard Griffith puts it in his book, *God in Man's Experience*, 'for that is what it is all about. A single theme runs through this mighty anthem of praise – the theme of God's grace. "Grace" is one of those religious words which has been worn thin with overuse like an old coin . . . Grace means something extra in life, like the flowers and letters and get-well cards . . . a gracious thing . . . The grace of God means God's extra, the way He deals with us beyond our deserving, the good things He gives us, not because He has to give them, but because He wants to give them. That is what makes Him God. In His goodness to men He goes further than we are willing to go, He does for us what no other person would ever do, He is a God Who surpasses all our human limitations. He showed Himself to be that kind of God in the experience of the Hebrew Psalmist; and if there is a single admonition that can be inferred from the one hundred and third Psalm, it is this: "Don't underestimate God!"'

That puts it beautifully. But turning now to the Psalm itself, as it appears in the Authorized Version (the word 'gracious' comes in the eighth verse):

Bless the Lord, O my soul:
And all that is within me, bless his holy name.
Bless the Lord, O my soul,
And forget not all his benefits:
Who forgiveth all thine iniquities;
Who healeth all thy diseases;
Who redeemeth thy life from destruction;
Who crowneth thee with lovingkindness and tender mercies;
Who satisfieth thy mouth with good things;
So that thy youth is renewed like the eagle's.
The Lord executeth righteousness
And judgement for all that are oppressed.
He made known his ways unto Moses,
His acts unto the children of Israel.
The Lord is merciful and gracious,
Slow to anger, and plenteous in mercy.
He will not always chide:
Neither will he keep his anger for ever.
He hath not dealt with us after our sins;
Nor rewarded us according to our iniquities.
For as the heaven is high above the earth,
So great is his mercy toward them that fear him.
As far as the east is from the west,
So far hath he removed our transgressions from us.
Like as a father pitieth his children,
So the Lord pitieth them that fear him.

For he knoweth our frame;
He remembereth that we are dust.
As for man, his days are as grass:
As a flower of the field, so he flourisheth.
For the wind passeth over it, and it is gone;
And the place thereof shall know it no more.
But the mercy of the Lord is from everlasting
  to everlasting upon them that fear him,
And his righteousness unto children's children;
To such as keep his covenant,
And to those that remember his commandments
  to do them.
The Lord hath prepared his throne in the heavens;
And his kingdom ruleth over all.
Bless the Lord, ye his angels,
That excel in strength, that do his commandments,
Hearkening unto the voice of his word.
Bless ye the Lord, all ye his hosts;
Ye ministers of his, that do his pleasure.
Bless the Lord, all his works
In all places of his dominion:
Bless the Lord, O my soul.

(Psalm 103:1–22, AV)

But the beautiful word 'Grace' is more distinctive of the New Testament, which always carries through the best that we have learned of God in the Old Testament – even in this lovely Psalm – to what more we see revealed in Jesus Christ. So we leave our public act of worship and go back into the world of daily service, with the words of the ancient benediction in our ears: 'The Grace of our Lord Jesus Christ, and the love of God, and the fellowship of the Holy Spirit be with us all now and ever. Amen.'

Added to this, in our daily service there is the need that, within our human limits, we must show this same Grace, this being and giving which is a gracious extra.

At the other end of the social scale, for balance, Michael Fairless tells of an old roadworker, and of the day on which there came to him the village Magdalene. She was hungry. He asked her to go away a distance until he had finished his meal, and then come and take what was left. But then his heart smote him, and he called her back, bidding her come and take what was there. He would then have anything that was left. So was added, that day, the grace of one old soul towards another!

A Time Of Stress

No life is wholly without its time of stress. The Psalmist stands close when he admits as much, in unforgettable words:

> Blessed be the Lord,
> for he has wondrously shown his steadfast love to me
> when I was beset as in a besieged city.
> I had said in my alarm,
> 'I am driven far from thy sight.'
> But thou didst hear my supplications,
> *when I cried to thee for help . . .*
>
> (Psalm 31:21–24, RSV)

One knows that these are not easy words – a great deal of experience lies within them.

After this lapse of time it is impossible to know what the Psalmist's troubles were, but we do know that they added up to great stress. He felt himself as in 'a besieged city'. And who among us has not at some time or other known a like experience, though we live in a century far removed from that of the Psalmist.

Merfyn Temple humbly tells of her own desperate experience, in *The Rain on the Earth.* (Seek out her book, if you have opportunity, for she has something to share that can spell a precious discovery for very many of us, in a time of stress.) It cannot be an identical experience, but it may be compounded of a like sense of loneliness, despair or incapacity. Says Merfyn Temple, thankfully: 'I thought I should never be able to carry on alone. But each day I seemed to get a new ration of strength from somewhere.' As a missionary in Northern Rhodesia (now Zimbabwe), she had long learned to lean on the prayers of others afar – but, most of all, on the presence of God, near at hand.

She found that her experience broke up into two parts: the first, a time of stress, and then, just as real, a time of deliverance. To realize the steadfast love and presence of God in that hour, was enough. *She did not lastingly falter nor fail, but triumphed in God.*

And to match the re-assurance of this woman of our day, with that of a man of our day, we can instance Dr Martin Luther King. His was such a daily, strong, splendid faith, that we might mistakenly imagine that problems automatically resolved themselves for him. But it was not so – just as the Psalmist assures us that such was not his own case – and you and I have no right to imagine anything of the kind happening to us. Whilst public feeling was cruelly confused, Martin Luther King was awakened by the telephone one night. At the other end was an angry voice saying loudly: 'Listen, nigger, we've taken all we want from you. Before next week, you'll be sorry you ever came to this town.' (Its threat was the harder for coming in the middle of the night, when it had to be answered by a weary campaigner, wakened from sleep.) It was just one more of the abusive calls which were his all-too-common experience then. Martin Luther King went through into the kitchen of his home, made himself a cup of coffee, and began to think calmly of his position, and what his alternatives were.

At last, he bowed his head over the table, and prayed aloud, saying: 'Lord, I am taking a stand for what I believe to be right. The people are looking to me for leadership, and if I stand before them without strength and courage, they will falter. I am at the end of my power. I have nothing left. I have come to the point where I can't face it alone.' And what happened? To put it briefly: that which happened to the Psalmist, to Merfyn Temple, and to many others up through the years of this complex thing we call life. Later Martin Luther King spoke of his experience to Coretta, his wife: 'At that moment I experienced the presence of the Divine as I had never experienced Him before. It seemed as though I could hear the quiet assurance of an inner voice saying, "Stand up for righteousness, stand up for truth; and God will be at your side forever."'

By what I can gather from the Psalmist, and from these splendid moderns, it seems wholly unlikely that their common experience of God, which made all the difference in their time of stress, was an emergency faith. It was, rather, something built up through all the years – so that when the need was pressing, God's delivering, sustaining, loving power was ready at hand.

Nor was it a faith limited to an awareness of God in the place of worship, though it must have been nourished there. It was a reality in the immediate secular setting of life, because it was not just a theoretical or theological pressure, but was involved in issues all-important at the very heart of life.

And it was something that had to be faced alone, as one judges the Psalmist's experience was; and certainly, Merfyn Temple's was; and Martin Luther King's was.

The Psalmist's words about God's 'steadfast love', breathe a great and sustaining confidence: '*Thou didst hear my supplications, when I cried to thee for help.*' In each case, an exultant assurance was added to life for all time. Whatever the pressures, there would always be that unforgettable memory of deliverance in God's presence.

And so real was it, that Merfyn Temple and Martin Luther King each delighted in it, urging on the rest of us, as does the Psalmist in his turn:

> Love the Lord, all you his saints!
> The Lord preserves the faithful . . .

Be strong, and let your heart take courage,
All you who wait for the Lord!
(Psalm 31:23–24, RSV)

I am glad that others have followed the Psalmist, for there is nothing in life's stress like God's 'steadfast love'.

Steadfast love takes no holidays!

This Very Day

It's a delight to think back to a four o'clock tea in Melbourne, with my fellow author Dr Frank Boreham. We had long corresponded, had both served the same publishing house, but we had not met. The Doctor had just finished a popular weekday service, and I had come from speaking in a nearby town. And good talk we had together! His most lively story was of a college-time experience, which something in our talk brought forward.

I learned how he had been sent to a Sussex village, to conduct the chapel anniversary on the following day. He was billetted with an an old lady, the widow of a former minister, a woman of faith, and a gracious hostess. She lived in a cottage nearly smothered with a tangle of creepers. They shared a meal, and an hour or two later retired, in view of the full day to follow. The young preacher found that he had been given his hostess's room, the best in the house. Everything had been done for his comfort, and he settled to a good sleep.

First thing next morning, he sprang out of bed, and pulled up the blind. As he did so, he noticed some words on the windowpane: THIS IS THE DAY. They did not immediately offer meaning, and he decided to ask his hostess, when they met at breakfast, how the words got there.

They were scratched on to the glass, and she herself had put them there. For a long time, she confessed, she had been worried about certain matters, and fearful often of what the days might bring. Then, she chanced to read a Psalm – and came across the verse: '*This is the day which the Lord hath made; we will rejoice and be glad in it*' (Psalm 118:24, AV). At once, she did her best to try to find out what day the

Psalmist meant. But there was nothing there to supply a hint, much less an answer. So she made up her mind that the day which was meant was that very day in which the Psalmist was living; and – when she spoke those words for herself – the very day in which she was living. The reality of it seemed so wonderful that she took up an old glasscutter, and cut four of the words on to her windowpane: THIS IS THE DAY. Thereafter, she looked out on to each new day, as it came, through that truth: 'THIS IS THE DAY which the Lord hath made; we will rejoice and be glad in it.' Work day, or worship day, it made no difference!

In early times no day had a name, it was just the period of daylight between sunrise and sunset. Later a measurement of the day in hours was introduced, and the naming of each day in honour of a national deity. (We still have a reminder of these.) This, of course, could not be undertaken until a simple timepiece had been invented for measuring hours, and a simple calendar for recording the passing days could be devised. The Psalmist lacked these – but he knew that each fresh day came from God, and he said so: 'This is the day which the Lord hath made . . .' To say as much was a secret of strength to him. He was able to believe that whatever happened to him that day, concerned God. He was able to add: 'We will rejoice and be glad in it!'

And this became the life-secret of Dr Boreham's old hostess, making an undreamed of difference to her anxieties and general fears. She was glad that no *one* day was mentioned; for she could recognize God's gift in *each* day.

(At one time, people worshipped God especially on the seventh day, as the celebration of the Creation; but when the New Testament era dawned, a change was made to the first day, the day of Christ's triumph over Death. Pliny the Elder, a Roman writer of history (AD 23–79), noted this change and was impressed. Many others, less learned, also noticed the worship custom of the early Christians. And many joined them. They called their day of public worship 'The Lord's Day'. But thereafter, every day, in a new sense, became the Lord's day!)

Curiously, many people are content to express what faith they have in terms of the past tense: 'good old times'. Many, who do not deliberately keep the seventh day holy instead of the first, have long since become despondent about these times, and about their contemporaries. 'In the good old days,' they persuade themselves, 'children always obeyed their elders; education taught things that were important; church pews were filled; and preaching was preaching then.'

But it would be folly to disregard some of the records available. 'A papyrus of 3000 BC,' Professor Morris of Bristol University reminds us, 'reads: "Young people are not what they used to be!"' But that is to move far into the past tense. A long time on, one Peter the Monk – a man we can surely depend on – found himself admitting: 'The young people of today think of nothing but themselves. They have no reverence for parents or old age. They are impatient of all restraint. They talk as if they knew everything, and what passes for wisdom with us is foolishness with them. As for the girls, they are forward and immodest, and unwomanly in speech, behaviour, and dress.' (How like an item in our daily newspaper it all seems!) In search of a more hopeful note, I jump to John Wesley, nearer our own times. Of his own 'past time', he writes: 'It is very hard that neither a sense of duty, nor all my thundering from the pulpit, can persuade young ladies and gentlemen to visit a poor person in the finest summer evening; while those very same delicate and time-loving young people will spend a whole night in dancing, which must be an exercise equal to walking many miles.' Flying from so distant a past, others will speak of days when servants were easily had, and 'service' was an accepted reality for many growing up. Now the inference is that those who can work for others, think only of their pay packets. And one need not go far to find instances that seem to suggest that in 'the past tense', everything was better, even amongst the working class, not to think of the most delicately brought up. But even then, there were terribly harsh living conditions to think of: the poorest, most meanly paid; daily toil of a harsh kind; and people hounded before the law without much sense of respect; education only possible for the highly privileged.

Others hold their religious faith in terms of the future tense, as they hold much else in life. To begin early in this mood, one says: 'When I am a big girl'; 'When I leave school'; 'When I start work, and get some money'; 'When I get married'; 'When the children are off my hands'; 'When the mortgage is paid off'; 'When I get the pension' – all in the future tense. 'When the political situation improves', says another; 'When we move from here'; 'When we get our new minister.' When, when, when!

But if life and religion is to be anything worthwhile, it needs to be in the present tense: '*This is the day which the Lord hath made; we will rejoice and be glad in it*' – the present tense!

The early American preachers were nicknamed '*The Now Men*' – and what better name could they have carried either in ridicule, or in tribute? They must have read the Psalmist's words; certainly, they were familiar with that one little word in the New Testament: '*Now* is the accepted time; behold, now is the day of salvation' (2 Corinthians 6:2, AV). 'Beloved, now are we the sons of God' (1 John 3:2, AV). Again: '*Now* we see not yet all things put under him. But we see Jesus' (Hebrews 2:8–9, AV).

Canon Raven, familiar with all these, and more, knows the importance of 'the present tense' for us, as vitally as did the Psalmist long ago. Says he, very tellingly for us: 'It is here and now, in the furnace, that the Son of God is discovered; in the valley of the shadow that His presence is our strength; in the face of Death that the gate of Life is opened.'

In Forgiveness

Someone at the time made a terrible comment on Queen Caroline's death: 'An unforgiving, unforgiven dies.' But it's not only at death that forgiveness is of great importance – it is, as the Psalmist suggests, in life. 'Blessed,' said he – or more tellingly rendered, 'happy' – 'is he whose transgression is forgiven, whose sin is covered' (Psalm 32:1, RSV). Transgression, at heart, implies wilful disobedience to a divine command. And the Psalm goes on to say: 'Blessed is the man to whom the Lord imputes no iniquity.'

And the Psalmist hasn't yet said all that he wants to say. He goes on to speak of deceit, meaning the fault of deception, and we all have some experience of that. We have all tried, at some time, to evade obligation. The Psalmist will not have us run the risk of missing out on this most valuable living and dying experience. So his message, translated into our tongue, reads:

Blessed is he whose transgression is forgiven,
whose sin is covered.
Blessed is the man to whom the Lord imputes no iniquity,
and in whose spirit there is no deceit.

When I declared not my sin, my body wasted away
through my groaning all day long.
For day and night thy hand was heavy upon me;
my strength was dried up as by the heat of summer.

I acknowledged my sin to thee,
and I did not hide my iniquity;
I said 'I will confess my transgressions to the Lord';
then thou didst forgive the guilt of my sin.

Therefore let every one who is godly
offer prayer to thee;
at a time of distress, in the rush of great waters,
they shall not reach him.
Thou art a hiding place for me,
thou preservest me from trouble;
thou dost encompass me with deliverance.

I will instruct you and teach you
the way you should go;
I will counsel you with my eye upon you.
Be not like a horse or a mule, without understanding,
which must be curbed with bit and bridle,
else it will not keep with you.

Many are the pangs of the wicked;
but steadfast love surrounds him who trusts in the Lord.
Be glad in the Lord, and rejoice, O righteous,
and shout for joy, all you upright in heart!

This is one of the penitential Psalms, added to 6, 38, 51, 102, 130 and 143. It quickly reveals the belief of the time that suffering was the outcome of one's transgressions. New light came later, when our Lord talked of sin and, as He did so, referred to those upon whom the Tower of Siloam fell. 'Think ye,' said He, 'that they were sinners above all men that dwelt in Jerusalem? I tell you, Nay!' (Luke 13:4–5, AV). It was long after the Psalmist's time that men and women learned that suffering, like rain, falls on the just and the unjust. Otherwise, religion could become an insurance policy – it would pay to live righteously. We know why much of our suffering comes, though not all. We are bound up together in the bundle of life, *drawing on unearned good and unearned ill.* If a father soaks his wits in drink, his family can hardly avoid suffering; but there is also the unwitting breach of health laws; and in this world of material things, it is very easy to slip on a wet step, or spill scalding liquids. Certainly, suffering bears no link to transgression – and that is on the authority of our Lord.

Whatever the origin of sin, to have it forgiven – and to be ourselves forgiving – is one of the greatest secrets of life. It was so in the Psalmist's day, and so centuries on in the life of John Wesley, acknowledging the New Testament condition set down in the Lord's Prayer: 'Forgive us, as we forgive.' Wesley could write in his diary, as a transforming discovery: '*I knew God for Christ's sake had forgiven me.*'

Forgiveness is the act by which God brings us back one by one, whatever the offence, into a right relationship with Himself, and with our fellow men. And the initiative is with Him: this is an undeserved favour, offered from His side. It is nothing that one can earn; no assurance that can be bought. Unless help comes from our forgiving God we are at a loss to lay hold on any kind of renewal. It seems too good to be true. But this reality is life-changing. Dr H. R. Mackintosh is undeniably right, in his summing-up in *The Christian Experience of Forgiveness*: 'Forgiveness is emphatically more than the ignoring of a trespass.'

> 'Tis sweet to stammer one letter
> of the Eternal's language
> on earth; it is called *Forgiveness*.

Though forgiveness is one of life's great discoveries, there are some things that forgiveness cannot do. The actual deeds of the unhappy past remain, of course – the health lost by the alcoholic father is still lost; the neighbour's house burned to the ground in a rage is still burned. These happenings are now facts of human life that have entered into history, and we have to recognize this.

Also the offender's disposition may well remain. Forgiveness does not automatically cast out a drinker's craving, or the hidden spite of the man with a match. But both may go on to know the grace of God's power to handle whatever human weakness they show.

The remembrance of former misdoings remains, too. Paul, the apostle, found this, all through the on-going ministry of his life in the early Church. Although he knew forgiveness, he could never forget that he had been a blasphemer and persecutor, who had opposed Christ. He always found it painful to remember this that he had done to Him. Men and women whom he had banished were still banished, many of them to far distant towns and waste places (1 Timothy 1:13, AV).

It is essential that one should receive the forgiveness offered. But before that, it is necessary that one should know that he needs it. (Some while after the bombing of Coventry Cathedral, I stood in that famous holy place. Christian worship had been carried on there for nine hundred years, but now its cathedral windows were out, and its gaunt walls against the sky showed how it had originally been dreamed five and a half centuries before. The rubble and wooden debris about the floor had already been gathered up, and a plan was being made to sow a short lawn of grass there. The remains of the altar window stood silhouetted against the sky. But even more telling was the Coventry Cross; the cross of silver-plated nails, standing against a great cross made of two charred beams. And below there stood, chiselled deep into the sanctuary stone, two words: FATHER FORGIVE. Just two words – but they were the words of Jesus on His Cross, words that no one standing there where I stood in Coventry, could ever forget.

(Some time later, I made another journey to Britain, and again to Coventry. Much had taken place in the meantime, although perhaps nothing more significant than something

Stephen Verney told me. The new Coventry Cathedral was now consecrated, and thousands of visitors, like myself, walked that way, among them a certain husband and wife. He was in origin a German, she, a Greek. With others, they were shown round the new cathedral, and took part in a service. After it all – notably the singing, preaching and praying – the wife said: 'I'm sorry, I can't speak . . . If only it were true!' And she burst into tears. 'But it was true!' commented Stephen Verney.) And it is still true. Like many of us, they had found themselves confronted not only by that inscription 'Father Forgive!' but by a realization that it was not only a piece of strikingly beautiful symbolism, but that *forgiveness is the only way in which men and women, and sinning nations, can come together in new life.*

In Silence

As a speaker, moving from gathering to gathering through the years, both in my own country and overseas, I've had my share of thanks for speaking. But only once have I ever shared thanks for silence. It happened one Sunday afternoon, in the Concert Chamber of our Town Hall. A warmhearted company of devotees of Madam Lili Kraus had gathered to spend an afternoon together.

Years before, she had first come to us from three harrowing years in a Japanese prisoner-of-war camp in Java. She had meant to begin a world tour, setting out from the Dutch East Indies, but in a painful, round-about way, had got to New Zealand. And we were, every one of us, richer for that.

Born in distant Budapest, she had started her devotion to the piano as a slight child of six. At eight, she had enrolled at the Royal Academy of Music, where among her teachers were the world-figures Zoltan Kodaly and Bela Bartok. At seventeen, she had earned the Academy's highest award. Soon she was pursuing studies under Edward Steurmann and Artur Schnabel at the Vienna Conservatory of Music. In three more years, she had become a fully-fledged professor, and in the years that followed, one of the most sought after recitalists in Europe. She toured, as guest with symphony orchestras, in England, in China, Japan, Australia, and in my own country.

After her grim prisoner-of-war experience, she came to us, with her growing family. She played, like a big sister to our students whenever they could gather. She played to enrich those others of us who gathered, and to raise funds for countries in need. She played with rare sensitivity, and utter self-giving. New Zealand later gave her citizenship, and from that day to this, she has enjoyed travelling on a New Zealand passport.

It couldn't have been an easy time for one of her musical gifts. But soon she was travelling alone, following her husband's death. Their family was by this time fully engaged in its own learning. Lili Kraus became the first artist in New York's musical history to perform all twenty-five of the great Mozart piano concerti; as well as to record the Complete Mozart Album.

And here she was again, after having been royally honoured, and in England granted the privilege of playing in Canterbury Cathedral; and, as opportunity came, having played to Dr Albert Schweitzer, in Lambarene.

But it is this one Sunday afternoon, when she played with grace and beauty to an unexpected company, that I remember always. She looked so beautiful, and so happy, tripping on to the platform to greet us as 'dear friends', and to speak briefly before each offering she made. The art of communication very quickly welded artist and audience into one. It was an enthralling experience, never to be forgotten.

And as the afternoon advanced, she commenced one of her several spoken introductions with something very striking: '*Thank you for the superb silences.*' Not a throat was cleared, not a cough broke through, not a programme rustled. The applause spelled out our appreciation – and so did the silences. We were locked in mutual delight – moved beyond all expectation.

When finally she returned to the platform, as if desiring to give us all that was humanly possible, she stood in silence, before she gracefully took her leave, her last words to us being: 'The Lord bless you, and keep you, and give you joy!'

And so we moved back into life, knowing ourselves truly blessed! Silence can do that – though all too seldom do we give it a chance.

Generally speaking, we are noisy most of the time. Robert Lynd, the British essayist, used to say: 'Mankind abhors a silence.' It does seem so. In addition to unnecessary talk – even before and after a service of worship – our life is attended by noise and clamour. We greet each other, and chat freely, often about next to nothing. Actually, the old Hebrew word *Sabbath* comes from a root meaning 'Stop doing what you are doing'. The late beloved Pope John spoke to Catholics and Protestants, alike, during the Ecumenical Council, when he said: 'We talk too much, and listen too little.'

Of one thing I am certain: great truth can only be born in great listening. (The Psalmist is not making any exception to this, when he says in the sixty-second Psalm, verse 5 (RSV): 'For God alone my soul waits in silence.')

Of how many of us is this true – and how often?

God has given us a world of Nature in which green trees, woods, streams and gardens offer us silent healing, and support. We need silence amid the tumultuous doings of the days we spend with others in work and play. All too often are we noisy, feverish or fussy. We do not understand what the Psalmist's words mean, or grasp their glorious importance: 'For God alone my soul waits in silence.'

Dr W. Russell Maltby knows us each better than many of us care to admit, when he writes:

ME: I am listening, Lord, for Thee; I am listening, Lord. (*Louder*) I am listening. (*Aside*: No one speaks. Is there anyone there?)
I am listening, Lord. (*Shouting*) I am listening.
VOICE: No! You're not.
ME: Yes, I am. I am listening, Lord.
VOICE: No! You're shouting.
ME: So I am. I won't shout any more. I'll be quiet. I am listening, Lord. I am listening, listening, listening. (*Aside*:

Nothing seems to happen.) I am listening, listening, listening.

VOICE: No, you're talking.

ME: Well, what must I do?

VOICE: Listen.

ME: Yes, but nothing happens when I do and I don't believe anything is going to happen.

VOICE: Oh, yes, something will happen.

ME: What?

VOICE: A nervous breakdown.

ME (*bitterly*): Yes, likely enough if I go on like this. Why is it so hard? Why is it so hard? I think I'll give it all up.

VOICE: He won't let you.

ME: Won't He? Well, I'll try again. I am listening, Lord. (*Pause*)

VOICE: Why are you in a hurry?

ME: I'm not – at least, am I? Still, I have a great deal to do and things are waiting, and – there isn't much time, and . . .

VOICE (*slowly*): You have all the time there is. What do you spend it on? You are not so busy as you think you are. You are frightened.

ME: Frightened? Frightened of what?

VOICE: Frightened of being alone. Frightened of remembering. Frightened of thinking of what I may say.

ME: Yes, I am. But what can I do?

VOICE: Perhaps nothing. Have you asked what I can do?

ME: What can You do?

VOICE: All that needs doing.

ME: Who are You?

VOICE: *I am the One you are running away from. Cease. Sit down and be at peace, and learn what I can do.*

The New Life Of Hope

It is a wonderful moment when one realizes that God's world is conceived in hope. Dawn follows darkness, Spring follows on the leaf-strewn way of Winter, the world is born anew with every little child, and resurrection awaits us beyond what we know as death.

Gratitude is on the lips of the Psalmist when he addresses God, as he delights to do:

> *O God of our salvation,*
> *Who art the Hope of all the ends of the earth.*
>
> (Psalm 65:5, RSV)

As he looks out, the Psalmist sees God's power and bounty all about him. It is not only a thing of the past, it is a thing of the future – and it enables him to go on.

We each in turn experience wintry days, when trees stand bare, and the sky is dark, the brightness of the sun hidden. The damp chill in our bones tends to make us sorry for ourselves.

But God does not leave us there – for God is a God of hope. His gift of Spring comes unfailingly, and we know it. It may be a little delayed, according to our calendar – but it never fails to appear. It's only a matter of days and hours. Then some retired neighbour – become nature-lover beyond the rest of us still heavily involved in the business of earning our living – points out in a neat letter to the Editor of *The Daily What's It*, that he has found the first crocus. A blackbird slinks through the shrubbery, busy with his own plans; a thrush is gathering odd straws to be added to a task undertaken with bird-like expectations of partner, eggs, and young – if one might not go so far as to call it hope. Young men, along with young women, pen love-poems; housewives turn to brooms and dusters, in a flurry of Spring-cleaning; husbands hunt out old paint-brushes and freshly chosen pots of paint, on their day off.

There is no holding oneself, or one's fellows – it is Spring! We know then what some call 'Spring madness', exchanging heavy garments for lighter; making plans for work, and leisure. And it happens every year when it's Spring! God has this delightful way, the world round, of bringing us a little further on into the miracle of hope. He can't help it – because He is the God of hope.

Caught up in what this season does for us all, one anonymous poet of our day speaks lightly of what Spring does for Nature:

How very glad the trees must be
Now that their leaves have come again
To greet the wind with ecstasy
And count the kisses of the rain.

When up and down the spiders run,
And to and fro the social bees
Are promenading in the sun,
Oh, how it must amuse the trees!

How they must love to hear the birds
Making a hundred thousand vows,
Filling the hours with lovely songs,
And hanging cradles in their boughs!

And this miracle of hope has its counterpart in our spirits. For we could never go on, without new beginnings – which is what hope spells for us faltering, sinning people. The wonder is that however deeply, foolishly we sin, there is hope for us, in God.

We can be more sure of this than could the Psalmist, although he delighted in God, because, living in the New Testament era, we have much to help us. Paul very early wrote to his friends – and so in turn to us – 'May the God of hope fill you with all joy and peace by your faith in him, until, by the power of the Holy Spirit, *you overflow with hope*' (Romans 15:13, NEB).

He is not limited to 'wishful thinking', to sentimentality – far from it; he can be as sure of God as was the Psalmist in his day, and more so. God's sustaining presence not only reaches out to him to the very rim of life here, but is as unlimited in the world to come. Of this, Paul has given us some of the greatest words of assurance, and we use them continually when death approaches, and also at the graveside, or in the crematorium service. '*If in this life only we have hope in Christ, we are of all men most miserable*. But now is Christ risen from the dead, and become the first fruits of them that slept. For since by man came death, by man came also the resurrection of the dead. For as in Adam all die, even so in Christ shall all be made alive' (1 Corinthians 15:19–22, AV).

> There is one glory of the sun, and another glory of the moon, and another glory of the stars; for one star differeth from another star in glory. So also is the resurrection of the dead. It is sown in corruption; it is raised in incorruption; it is sown in dishonour; it is raised in glory; it is sown in weakness; it is raised in power; it is sown a natural body; it is raised a spiritual body . . . And so it is written, The first man Adam was made a living soul; the last Adam was made a quickening spirit . . . Behold, I shew you a mystery: We shall not all sleep, but we shall all be changed . . . For this corruptible must put on

incorruption, and this mortal must put on immortality . . .
O death, where is thy sting? O grave, where is thy victory? The sting of death is sin; and the strength of sin is the law. But thanks be to God, which giveth us the victory through our Lord Jesus Christ.

(1 Corinthians 15:41–57, AV)

In *The Countryman*, Joan Youle tells of an old roadman supported by this reality. When a neighbour in a Radnorshire village offered his sympathies to him, on the death of one of his friends, the old man replied: 'Ah, 'twas very sad. 'E was workin' on same job as me any amount of times, breakin' stones up in the 'ills, I knowed 'im well. 'E was sittin' up in 'is sittins when I seed 'im last, but 'is time was wearin'. Ah, I shall miss 'im no odds. And in the 'ospital they woke 'im up at five every mornin' to wash 'im – all them sort o' capers. I couldn't go to the funeral, *but I went to the chapel and sang 'is soul over the 'ills.*'

Earth And Outer Space

The Psalmist would have been more amazed than any of us, could he have heard that a day would come when a man would set off into space. But on one important point, at least, he'd find himself akin. John Glenn, the astronaut, took off. None of us had ever experienced anything like it before, and nor had John Glenn. He was asked by journalists whether he felt a special need for God in that critical undertaking. Glenn replied that his religion was an integral part of his normal living, therefore he was not making an emergency appeal to God, since he was taking off into the loneliness of outer space. His was not an emergency religion only.

The Psalmist's attitude, as revealed in Psalm 73, was of two parts. At first he had settled little or no faith in God. (For how long we have no idea; but it gave him for life little or nothing.) But he spoke of it long afterwards:

> When my soul was embittered,
> when I was pricked in heart,
> I was stupid and ignorant,
> I was like a beast towards thee.
> (Psalm 73:21–22, RSV)

A change came – not the thing of a moment, but of a constant, well-tried attitude, over a length of testing. Then he could say as really as John Glenn:

> *Nevertheless I am continually with thee*;
> thou dost hold my right hand.
> Thou dost guide me with thy counsel,
> and afterward thou wilt receive me to glory.

Whom have I *in heaven* but thee?
And there is nothing *upon earth* that I desire
besides thee.
My flesh and my heart may fail,
but God is the strength of my heart
and my portion for ever.
(Psalm 73:23–26, RSV)

God remains the Psalmist's supporting presence and, sure of this, he delights to bear witness to Him. His words echo experience – something much more than an emergency could ever offer. 'God is the strength of my heart.'

The idea of running our own lives, with an occasional appeal to God for extra help when life faces us with more than we can manage alone, is not true religion, although all too many around us do take this attitude. Often in our daily lives, we buy something such as a TV set, a washing-machine, or a typewriter, with a guarantee for a certain stated time, so that if anything goes wrong we can call upon the maker or provider to put it right. We hope that won't be necessary, that we can manage on our own. All too many of us are liable to think of God like that – but not the Psalmist, and not John Glenn!

The maker of heaven and earth does not leave any of us who depend on Him constantly to our own devices. We would often be in a sorry way if He did. We do not find ourselves launching into outer space; but we do enter into new jobs, the building of homes, the raising of a family, the experience of grievous sickness, the responsibilities of public service, the involvement in various important decisions affecting the welfare of multitudes. We are all bound up in the bundle of life. We are all dependent on our creator and provider, God; He is the maker and provider of persons, as well as things, in this mighty universe. And it is impossible for any one of us to travel, even in these scientific days, *beyond His caring, loving presence.* This, undoubtedly, meant a great deal to John Glenn.

And it can do so for any one of us, wherever we are, faced with whatever comes. We are always seeking words to assure ourselves on this all important point. A contemporary Creed authorized by the United Church of Canada, offers us this assurance:

> Man is not alone, he lives in God's world.
> We believe in God:
>   Who has created and is creating,
>   Who has come in the true Man, Jesus, to
>   reconcile and make new,
>   Who works in us and others by His Spirit.
>   We trust Him.
>
>   He calls us to be His Church:
>   to celebrate His presence,
>   to love and serve others,
>   to seek justice and resist evil,
>   to proclaim Jesus, crucified and risen, our judge
>   and hope.
>
>   In life, in death, in life beyond death, God is with us,
>   We are not alone.
>
> Thanks be to God.

We moderns – in this New Testament era – have much on which to count for strength, which was completely unknown to the Psalmist. One of Paul's most famous certainties leads us on:

> He that spared not his own Son, but delivered him up for us all, how shall he not with him also freely give us all

> things? . . . Who shall separate us from the love of Christ? shall tribulation, or distress, or persecution, or famine, or nakedness, or peril, or sword? . . . Nay, in all these things we are more than conquerors through him that loved us. For I am persuaded, that neither death, nor life, nor angels, nor principalities, nor powers, nor things present, nor things to come, nor height, nor depth, nor any other creature, shall be able to separate us from the love of God, which is in Christ Jesus our Lord.
>
> (Romans 8:32–39, AV)

Added to this we have Christ's assurance: 'Lo, I am with you alway, even unto the end of the world' (Matthew 28:20, AV).

In Songs, And More Songs

The book of Psalms is for many of us the most familiar part of the Old Testament. Added to what we have already shared of its structure, there is another point which Dr Edgar Goodspeed puts as well as any scholar. 'As it stands,' he says, 'the book of Psalms may be described as the hymnbook and the prayerbook of the Second Temple – built in 520–516 BC by the Jewish exiles who returned to Jerusalem. It contains,' he underlines for us, 'some duplicates, certain psalms appearing in it more than once. (Thus Psalm 53 repeats Psalm 14; Psalm 70 repeats Psalm 40:14–17; and Psalm 108 consists of Psalm 57:7–11, and Psalm 60:5–12.)'

This ought in no way to surprise us, since these are collected out of life, for life – and life is like that, with many repetitions. It is the prayerbook of the people of the time – and prayers are like that. It is the songbook of the people of the time – and songs are like that.

Here and there one comes upon a deep sense of sin and guilt; elsewhere are appeals for God's help. In other Psalms, hope raises its head, trust comes alive, and gratitude finds words to express itself. With it all is a sense of God's closeness and personal care, a love of His law, and the whole thing climaxes by all within His glorious created world bursting into song.

These are all Psalms *lived* before ever they were written down or shared. Some are personal, expressed only between the singer and God. Others are sung in company in the Temple worship, or on pilgrimage. Sometimes, such simple musical instruments as they could gather, added to the total richness of sharing. In Psalm 150, the last, is a list of the instruments: the trumpet, the psaltery and harp, the timbrel, stringed instruments and organs, loud cymbals and high sounding cymbals. But this, at last, calls upon all the living: '*Let everything that hath breath praise the Lord!*' And it does not forget a personal challenge: '*Praise ye the Lord!*'

Dr Goodspeed lists Psalm 95, among others; and indeed, it is a longstanding favourite of many of us:

O come, let us sing unto the Lord:
Let us make a joyful noise to the rock of our salvation.
Let us come before his presence with thanksgiving,
And make a joyful noise unto him with psalms.
For the Lord is a great God,
And a great King above all gods.
In his hand are the deep places of the earth:
The strength of the hills is his also.
The sea is his, and he made it:
And his hands formed the dry land.
O come, let us worship and bow down:
Let us kneel before the Lord our maker.
For he is our God;
And we are the people of his pasture, and the sheep of his hand.
Today if ye will hear his voice,
Harden not your heart, as in the provocation,
And as in the day of temptation in the wilderness:
When your fathers tempted me,
Proved me, and saw my work.
Forty years long was I grieved with this generation,
And said, It is a people that do err in their heart,
And they have not known my ways:
Unto whom I sware in my wrath
That they should not enter into my rest.

(Psalm 95:1–11, AV)

A few Psalms on is the hundredth, and that begins in the same mood:

> Make a joyful noise unto the Lord, all ye lands.
> Serve the Lord with gladness:
> Come before his presence with singing.

Commonly called the *Jubilate*, its metrical version, composed by William Kethe, the sixteenth-century Scottish friend of John Knox, is the Psalm most commonly sung in Christian worship among us today, as

> All people that on earth do dwell,
> Sing to the Lord with cheerful voice . . .

Fletcher of Saltoun used to say: 'Let me make the songs of the country, and let who will, make the laws.' It was a bold statement, but he believed so greatly in the ministry of song. We cannot help but associate laws with disquietude in the family and community, not to say in the Church – whereas nothing is further from the idea of song. The witness of the centuries is to the worth of songs, and not least in the realm of religion.

Some think that our faith ought not to be signed but sung. And the Psalmist, all that long time ago, I think would have agreed with that. I frequently come upon memorial plaques in our churches, raised to keep alive gratitude for some great preacher; but I'm wondering now how needful they are – for a preacher is set there to preach. Lately, I came upon a remembrance in St Dunstan's-in-the-West, in London: *To an honest lawyer*. So there are memorials and memorials. One of the rarest I have ever come upon, in my own land – though it ought not to be rare – is in the beautiful little Putiki Memorial Church. It memorializes the services of 'Miss M. Tahana, choir soloist for many years'.

Turning from the Psalms to the New Testament era, I have been impressed by the fact that when, at the birth of Christ, God's best news came to our world, it came, not in a sermon – but in a *song*. The breakthrough reached humble men, shepherds in the fields by night, and set them on their way to seek out a Babe in Bethlehem. Some time on, Pliny reported to the Emperor that the most noticeable thing about the early Christians who cherished that Good News given first in the shepherd fields, was the way they kept singing in their little meeting places. Jerome, in turn, had a like story to tell: 'The ploughman at his plough,' said he, 'sings his joyful hallelujahs; the busy mower refreshes himself with Psalms; the vinedresser sings the songs of David.' And Chrysostom's words are similar: 'All come together with us to sing, and in it they unitedly join – the young and the old, the rich and the poor, women and men, slaves and free, all send forth one melody.' Centuries on, with John and Charles Wesley – gifted, and God-serving through preaching and song – it was the same. The Church was born – and re-born – in song! Moments of elation are best caught up in song!

In all ages, song has ennobled religion. At the close of a service of worship, one old Welsh soul is remembered to have said: 'Ah, yes, but he ought to have sung the last part of the sermon!' Certainly song can rise where spoken words are powerless to go. I believe that all realities sing. The poet Lascelles Abercrombie is not far from the truth moving many of the Psalmists, when he says:

Crumble, crumble,
voiceless things,
No faith can last,
that never sings!

A Crescendo Of Praise

Many stories, many songs, many services have a way of petering out as they reach their end, but this is not the experience of those of us who spend time with the Psalmists. There are confessions of grief, of bewilderment and failure – but the whole actually ends in a splendid paean of praise. The one hundred and fifty songs start to ascend to that high point with the one hundred and forty-sixth:

> *Praise the Lord!*
> Praise the Lord, O my soul!
> I will praise the Lord as long as I live;
> I will sing praises to my God while I have being.
>
> (Psalm 146:1–2, RSV)

But that is not all that stirs within the heart of the Psalmist. In the next Psalm, he adds to that even greater praise:

> *Praise the Lord!*
> For it is good to sing praises to our God;
> For he is gracious, and a song of praise is seemly.
>
> (Psalm 147:1, RSV)

But that is not all. The Psalmists look up above any human experience, and add to what has been already said:

> *Praise the Lord!*
> Praise the Lord from the heavens, praise him in the heights!
> Praise him, all his angels, praise him, all his host!
>
> (Psalm 148:1–2, RSV)

Then the Psalmists turn to the worshippers who regularly assemble to remember, and gather up remembrance of God's goodness:

> *Praise the Lord!*
> Sing to the Lord a new song,
> His praise in the assembly of the faithful!
>
> (Psalm 149:1, RSV)

But the song still goes on, this time reaching the highest heights, as one powerless to do more than assemble what has been already said:

> *Praise the Lord!*
> Praise God in his sanctuary;
> praise him in his mighty firmament!
> Praise him for his mighty deeds;
> praise him according to his exceeding greatness!
>
> Praise him with trumpet sound;
> praise him with lute and harp!
> Praise him with timbrel and dance;
> praise him with strings and pipe!
> Praise him with sounding cymbals;
> praise him with loud clashing cymbals!
> Let everything that breathes praise the Lord!
> Praise the Lord!
>
> (Psalm 150:1–6, RSV)

So end the Psalms, as presented to us, with a crescendo of praise: humble men and women of the earth taking part, and every living creature gathered in, to mount up with sound, commanding all that musicians can offer, and everything on earth, and above, journeying on. This is praise *in excelsis*!

The only compulsion God the Eternal puts upon us is His

own praise-worthiness of nature, and His acts. Then it is left to us. And knowing Him for what He is, we cannot refrain from praise – praise that with that of the Psalmist, ever and ever more rises to a mighty crescendo! He alone, Who sets the world swinging in space, the sun and Orion on their stately march, and paves the Milky Way with millions of worlds, is worthy of such praise!

To earth's wonders enumerated by the Psalmist, we of the New Testament era are bound to add the miracle of our redemption. We cannot bypass Bethlehem, Nazareth, and the Open Tomb in a Garden in Jerusalem; nor the hill hard by where, at Christ's command, His friends gathered to take bodily leave of Him, listening to His injunction: 'Go ye . . . and teach all nations, baptizing them in the name of the Father, and of the Son, and of the Holy Ghost: teaching them to observe all things whatsoever I have commanded you: and lo, I am with you alway, even unto the end of the world' (Matthew 28:19–20, AV).

'It can't be by accident,' added Dr Erik Routley, an experienced leader of praise, in our day, 'that the word for "Praise" in any language is always a fine word for singing: "Praise the Lord *Louez Dieu – Lobe den Herren – Laudate Dominum – Euligeite Theon – Hallelujah!"* They are words of full vowels and strong consonants, words that exercise the muscles of the mouth and throat, and the strength of piety to their utmost.'

Be Thou my dignity, Thou my delight!
(Ancient Hymn)

Acknowledgements

The author is grateful for permission to use the following material:

'Where are you going, shepherd?', and 'I am listening, Lord', Dr William Russell Maltby, *Obiter Scripta* – Selected and arranged by Francis B. James; Epworth Press, 1952.

'Come, Sweetheart, listen . . .' Poem by John Drinkwater from *Collected Poems, Vol. 1, 1908–1917*; Sidgwick & Jackson Ltd; p.77.

Heterodoxy – poem by the late Teresa Hooley.

'God of distances . . .' Poem-prayer by my late friend, Jane Merchant.

Other quotations are either fully acknowledged in the text, out of copyright or, where no source is given, by Rita Snowden herself.